THE **ADLARD COLES** BO

HULL & DECK
REPAIR

DON CASEY

ADLARD COLES NAUTICAL
LONDON

CONTENTS

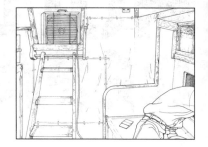

INTRODUCTION:

BEAUTY IS MORE THAN SKIN DEEP

Fiberglass.

Legendary yacht designer L. Francis Herreshoff has—somewhat inelegantly, it seems to me—called this versatile material "frozen snot." Maybe so, but how many of Herreshoff's beautiful wooden boats have ended up as lobster condominiums or fuel for a boat shed stove, while snot-built boats of the same age, no matter how undeserving of immortality, continue to ply the world's oceans, bays, and estuaries? Wooden boats regularly die early deaths of natural causes; fiberglass boats must be assassinated.

Don't get me wrong; I love wooden boats, and in particular I love Herreshoff's wooden boats. There is something magical about taking straight lumber and manipulating it into the flowing contours of a boat. The craftsmanship of the builder is obvious: planks steamed to linguini and worried into compound curves, knees cut from a natural crook to harness the tree's full strength, precise dovetail joints wedding shelf and beam. Such craft is far less evident in a hull formed by painting a boat-shaped mold with a thick layer of fiber and sticky glop. That the dried glop pops out of the mold with the same graceful curves yields no redemption.

But it isn't redemption that is called for; it's perspective. If we open the leaded glass doors in the galley of one of Mr. Herreshoff's classic wooden yachts, we are likely to encounter fine china. Why not wooden plates, woven bowls? Because china dishes—molded bone-reinforced clay—are infinitely more serviceable.

Likewise molded glass-reinforced plastic boats.

Fiberglass is malleable, durable, and easy to maintain. These characteristics, widely known, have made fiberglass the overwhelming material of choice for boat construction for more than three decades. If you want a boat to display, wood has much to recommend it, but for a boat to *use*, fiberglass is hard to beat.

A lesser-known virtue of fiberglass is that it is easy to repair. A fiberglass hull's seamless nature leads many boatowners to conclude that repair must be difficult. Any assertion to the contrary too often elicits raised eyebrows. In the pages that follow, we hope to quell the skeptics with astoundingly clear explanations, but the only way you can fully purge yourself of any nagging doubts is to buy a can of gelcoat paste or a bit of glass cloth and resin and give it a whirl. You'll wonder what you were worried about.

While this book is confined to hull and deck repairs to fiberglass boats, it is not limited to fiberglass repairs. Fiberglass boats are not *all* fiberglass. Decks, for example, may be cored with plywood, balsa, or foam, railed with aluminum, covered with teak, outfitted with bronze, interrupted with acrylic, penetrated with stainless steel, and booted with rubber. Virtually all of these components require regular maintenance and occasional repair, and they must be assembled properly and carefully if the boat is to be dry.

Watertight joints are our first order of business. Boatowners today don't need even a passing acquaintance with oakum caulking and firming irons; molded hulls are completely seamless, and rare is the fiberglass *hull* that leaks, no matter how old. Deck leaks are, unfortunately, another matter. The dirty little secret of fiberglass boats is that most are only slightly more watertight than a colander. Spray? Rain? Wash-down water? A significant amount of all three finds its way below.

Deck leaks don't just wet the contents of lockers, drip on bunks, and trickle across soles; they destroy wood core, corrode chainplates, and delaminate bulkheads. Identifying and eliminating leaks is essential. This book details the most effective technique for sealing joints and bedding hardware, and it provides specific sealant recommendations for various uses. It instructs you in portlight replacement, hull-to-deck joints, and centerboard trunk repairs. It also shows you how to test your work and how to locate pesky leaks.

Often all that is wrong with a fiberglass hull is a chalky surface or a few scratches. Restoring the gloss can be the easiest of repairs to fiberglass; it is where we begin our exposition of this material.

The ravages of time affect decks more than hulls. An older fiberglass deck is likely to be webbed with hairline cracks, even pocked with open voids, and may have stress cracks radiating from corners or from beneath hardware. Fortunately there are easy ways to repair these blemishes. Step-by-step instructions for restoring the deck to perfection are provided.

Deck repairs are complicated by the necessity of providing effective nonskid surfaces. Owners of boats with molded-in nonskid will find the included instructions for renewing those surfaces useful. Those with planked decks will be more interested in the section detailing the care and repair of teak overlay.

Eventually, of course, a hull-and-deck-repair book for fiberglass boats must come around to repairs requiring fiberglass lay-up, but not without first providing clear and concise descriptions of the various materials to be used. When should you use polyester resin and when epoxy? What is vinylester? Cloth, mat, or roving? You will find answers to these questions and more in Chapter 4.

Armed with an understanding of the materials involved and guided by clear illustrations, you are ready to take on more complicated repairs. Chapter 5 shows you how to repair deck delamination and how to replace spongy core. Chapter 6 focuses on hull repairs—dealing with gouges, repairing blisters, and reconstructing after impact damage. A quick look in Chapter 7 at repairing common rudder and keel problems, and you will have taken the cannon.

When all boats were built of wood, a truly professional repair required the skills of someone with years of experience. Not so with fiberglass. Pay attention and give it a try, and you will discover that there is virtually no repair to a fiberglass hull or deck that a motivated owner can't do as well (if not as quickly) as a pro.

Frozen snot, indeed!

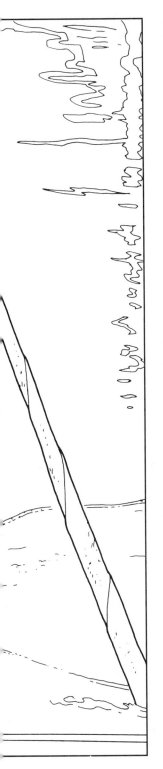

LEAKS

Leaks are insidious. A tiny leak, left unattended for months or years, can easily result in damage that will cost thousands of dollars to have repaired, or take innumerable hours if you make the repairs yourself.

There are the obvious things: ruined interior varnish below leaking ports, mildewed upholstery from trickles from the hull-to-deck joint, a punky cabin sole from "mysterious" rainwater intrusion.

As serious as these are, they're small potatoes. The biggest risk from leaks is to the deck core, and you may not see any evidence of a leak until major damage is already done.

The decks of most fiberglass boats are made up of a plywood or balsa core sandwiched between two skins of fiberglass. (Closed-cell foam, more resistant to saturation but no less susceptible to delamination, is found in relatively few production boats.) If water penetrates the fiberglass skin and gets into the core, the result is likely to be failure of the bond between the core and the skin(s). This core delamination weakens the deck. Delamination is accelerated if the boat is subjected to temperatures that cause the trapped water to freeze and expand.

The water entering a cored deck cannot get back out; the flow is one way, like filling a jug. Balsa cores become saturated and mushy. Plywood soon rots. In both cases, the only solution is cutting away the fiberglass skin and replacing the core. After you do this job once, knowing full well that it could have been prevented with four-bits' worth of caulk and an hour's worth of effort, you will become religious about maintaining a watertight seal around any hole in the deck.

CHOOSING A SEALANT

You walk into a marine store and there they are, dozens of different cartridges and tubes standing on shelves, stacked in bins, and hanging in blister cards. Geez, how many different kinds of marine sealants can there be?

Three. That's it. Three. Understand these three and you have the selection process whipped.

POLYSULFIDE

Polysulfide is the Swiss Army knife in marine sealants; you can use it for almost everything. Often called Thiokol (a trademark for the polymer that is the main ingredient of all polysulfide sealants regardless of manufacturer), polysulfide is a synthetic rubber with excellent adhesive characteristics. As a bedding compound it allows for movements associated with stress and temperature change, yet maintains the integrity of the seal by gripping tenaciously to both surfaces. Polysulfide is also an excellent caulking compound since it can be sanded after it cures and it takes paint well.

Use polysulfide for everything except plastic. Polysulfide bonds as well to plastic surfaces as to any other, but the solvents in the sealant attack some plastics, causing them to harden and split. Specifically, don't use polysulfide to bed plastic portlights, either acrylic (Plexiglas) or polycarbonate (Lexan). Don't use it to bed plastic deck fittings (including portlight frames); plastic marine fittings are generally either ABS or PVC, and polysulfide will attack both. Any plastic fitting made of epoxy, nylon, or Delrin—such as quality plastic through-hull fittings—may be safely bedded with polysulfide.

The black caulking between the planks of a teak deck is polysulfide. For this application, a two-part polysulfide gives the best results. Because polysulfide adheres well to teak (a special primer improves adhesion), and because it is unaffected by harsh teak cleaners, it is also the best choice for bedding teak rails and trim.

Polysulfides are the slowest curing of the three types of sealant, often taking a week or more to reach full cure.

POLYURETHANE

Polyurethane is the bulldog of marine sealants—once it gets a grip, it doesn't turn loose. Polyurethane is such a tenacious adhesive that its bond should be thought of as permanent; if there is any likelihood that you will want to separate the two parts later, don't use polyurethane to seal them.

Use polyurethane anywhere you want a permanent joint. This is the best sealant for the hull-to-deck joint. It is also a good choice for through-hull fittings and for toerails and rubrails, but not if they are raw teak because some teak cleaners soften it. Like polysulfide, polyurethane should not be used on most plastics—acrylic, polycarbonate, PVC, or ABS.

The cure time for polyurethane is generally shorter than polysulfide, but still may be up to a week.

SILICONE

Silicone can seem like the snake oil of the marine sealant trio. A bead of this modern miracle is too often expected to cure any and every leak. And it

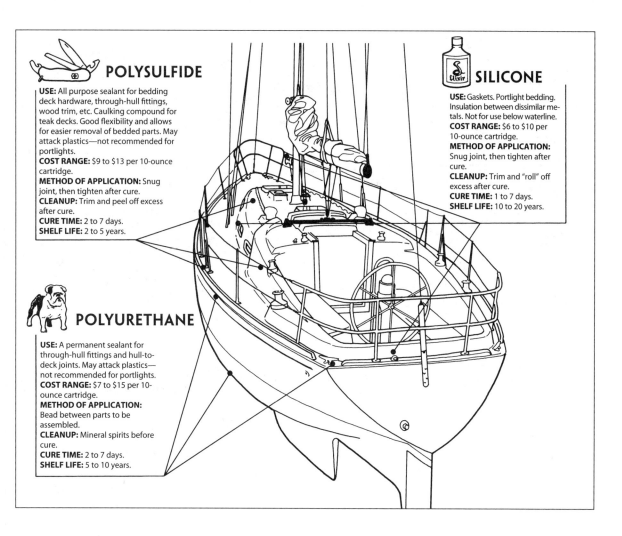

POLYSULFIDE

USE: All purpose sealant for bedding deck hardware, through-hull fittings, wood trim, etc. Caulking compound for teak decks. Good flexibility and allows for easier removal of bedded parts. May attack plastics—not recommended for portlights.
COST RANGE: $9 to $13 per 10-ounce cartridge.
METHOD OF APPLICATION: Snug joint, then tighten after cure.
CLEANUP: Trim and peel off excess after cure.
CURE TIME: 2 to 7 days.
SHELF LIFE: 2 to 5 years.

SILICONE

USE: Gaskets. Portlight bedding. Insulation between dissimilar metals. Not for use below waterline.
COST RANGE: $6 to $10 per 10-ounce cartridge.
METHOD OF APPLICATION: Snug joint, then tighten after cure.
CLEANUP: Trim and "roll" off excess after cure.
CURE TIME: 1 to 7 days.
SHELF LIFE: 10 to 20 years.

POLYURETHANE

USE: A permanent sealant for through-hull fittings and hull-to-deck joints. May attack plastics—not recommended for portlights.
COST RANGE: $7 to $15 per 10-ounce cartridge.
METHOD OF APPLICATION: Bead between parts to be assembled.
CLEANUP: Mineral spirits before cure.
CURE TIME: 2 to 7 days.
SHELF LIFE: 5 to 10 years.

does—for about as long as it used to take the magic elixir salesman to slip out of town. Then the bead releases its grip, and what started out as a tube full of promise ends up as a dangling rubber worm. All is not lost—with a hook and the right wrist action, you can at least catch dinner.

Silicone sealant is a gasket material—period. If you think of silicone's adhesive abilities as temporary at best, you will find it is the best product for a number of sealing requirements. It is the only one of the marine sealant trio than can be safely used to bed plastic. It is an excellent insulator between dissimilar metals—use it when mounting stainless hardware to an aluminum spar. It is the perfect gas-ket material between components that must be periodically dismantled—beneath hatch slides, for example.

Silicone retains its resilience for decades and is unaffected by most chemicals, but it should not be used below the waterline. Because it depends upon mechanical compression to maintain its seal, silicone is not the best choice for sealing hardware on a cored deck. Exposed silicone is a magnet for dirt but repels paint like an opposite pole, so never fillet with silicone, and don't use this sealant on any surface you plan to paint.

Silicone sealants typically set in a few minutes and usually reach full cure in less than 24 hours.

A USEFUL HYBRID

THERE IS A BIG ADVANTAGE TO USING A SEALANT with good adhesive properties. An adhesive sealant maintains its seal even when stresses pull or pry the bedded components apart, the sealant stretching and compressing like the bellows joining the two sides of an accordion.

This accordion effect would be especially useful for plastic portlight installations where the portlights are not bolted in place but rather clamped between an inner and outer frame. As the cabin sides expand and contract with temperature changes or flex with rigging stresses, the space between the frames varies.

Applied properly (see "Rebedding Deadlights"), silicone sealant can accommodate these variations, but it is not easy to set the portlight in a uniform thickness of silicone. Although silicone has amazing elasticity, its lack of adhesion means it must always be under pressure to maintain a watertight seal. If the gasket formed by the cured silicone is thin anywhere around the portlight, the seal is sure to fail, probably sooner rather than later.

Either polysulfide or polyurethane would provide a more dependable seal, but polysulfide is certain to attack the plastic, and polyurethane prohibits any future disassembly. Fortunately a chemist somewhere, one who undoubtedly owns a boat and tried to bed plastic portlights, cooked up a new goo that is part silicone and part polyurethane. Marketed by BoatLife as Life Seal, this is a more durable sealant than silicone for portlights and other plastic fittings.

REBEDDING DECK HARDWARE

Fiberglass boats are notorious leakers. Wood is, to a degree, self-sealing; a leak swells the wood, pinching off further leakage. Not so with fiberglass. Once the seal between the fiberglass and the hardware is broken, it will leak unabated until you reseal it. The seal can be broken by stress, by deterioration, or by temperature changes. Wrenching the top of a lifeline stanchion can break the seal at the base. Sunlight and chemicals erode sealants. In cold weather the deck may literally contract away from the hardware.

Every seal on the deck (and hull) of a fiberglass boat should be carefully examined at least annually, and at any sign of failure, the joint should be opened, cleaned, and resealed. This modest investment is guaranteed to return greater relative dividends than even your most profitable stock fund.

1 Gather all the necessary materials. If you are using a cartridge—economical if you have quite a bit of rebedding to do—you need a caulking gun. Have masking tape and adhesive cleaner on hand to control squeeze-out.

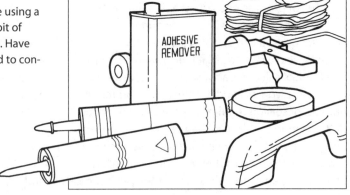

2 Remove the fitting. This is usually the hardest part of the job, either because access to the fasteners is difficult to gain or because the bolts are frozen—or both. Access sometimes requires removing headliners or cabinetry, but don't try to avoid this by simply running a bead of sealant around the fitting. If you do that, eventually you will still be removing the fitting, only this time in preparation for major deck repair.

For access to the fasteners securing wooden components, the bungs hiding the bolt heads will have to be removed. This can be accomplished by drilling a small hole in the center of the bung and threading a screw into it; when the point of the screw finds the screw head below the bung, continuing to turn the screwdriver will lift the bung. Extracting bungs this way can sometimes damage the bung hole. A safer method is to drill the bung with a bit slightly smaller than the diameter of the bung, then carefully remove the remaining ring of material with a small chisel.

If the fitting was installed with polyurethane, removing the fasteners may have little effect. Trying to pry the fitting loose is likely to result in damage to the deck and the fitting. Heating the fitting (especially metal fittings) or the deck can coax the polyurethane to release its grip.

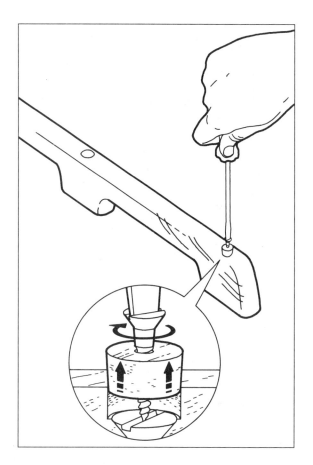

HEADLINERS

HEADLINERS ARE AS VARIED AS BOATS. If the headliner is fiberglass, you likely cannot remove it (without removing the deck). Occasionally manufacturers bolt hardware to the deck before installing it over the headliner. You will have to cut or drill the headliner beneath the fasteners to gain access. Reinstall the hardware with longer bolts through spacers and a backing plate that covers the cutout.

When the headliner is made up of panels, it is usually captured by trim pieces screwed in place. Panels may also attach with Velcro.

Sewn headliners are typically stapled to wooden strips across the overhead. You can't see the staples because they are through the excess material on the back side at the seams. You gain access by removing the trim piece at the forward or aft end of the liner and pulling the liner loose at that end. Work the staples out with a flat screwdriver at the seams until you uncover the desired area. Be sure you use Monel staples when you replace the liner. For more on headliners, see *Canvaswork and Sail Repair* in this series.

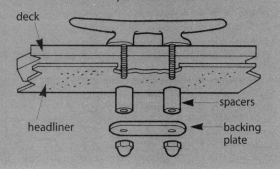

deck
headliner
spacers
backing plate

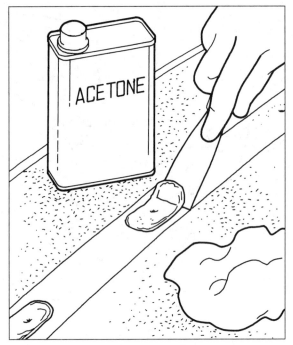

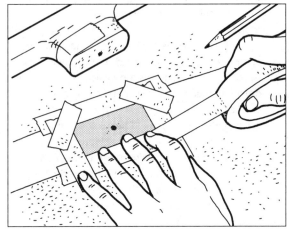

3 Clean off the old bedding. Every trace of the old sealant must be removed. Use a blade, sandpaper, or a wire brush as required, and clean both the deck and the fitting with acetone.

4 Mask adjacent areas. Cleaning up the squeeze-out with solvent takes twice as long as masking and is ten times more messy. Dry-fit the part and trace around it with a pencil. This is the time to strengthen the mounting location if required (see "Deck Repairs"). Mask the deck ⅛ inch outside the pencil line and mask the edge of the fitting.

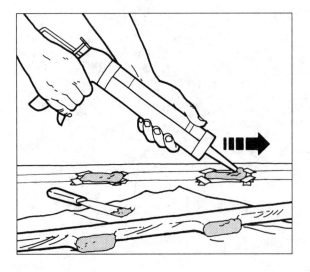

5 Coat both surfaces with sealant. Cut the tip of the tube or cartridge at a 45° angle—close to the tip for a thin bead, farther back for a thicker bead. (Cartridges have an inner seal you will have to puncture with an ice pick.) Apply the sealant with a forward motion, pushing the bead in front of the nozzle. Coat both surfaces to make sure there will not be any gaps in the bond; use a putty knife to spread the sealant evenly, like buttering bread. Before inserting the mounting bolts—not screws—run a ring of sealant around each just below the head. NEVER apply sealant around the fasteners on the underside of the deck; if the seal with the outer skin breaks, you want the water to pass into the cabin where it will be noticed.

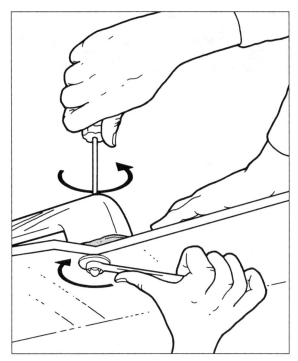

6 Assemble the parts and "snug" the fasteners enough to squeeze sealant out all the way around.

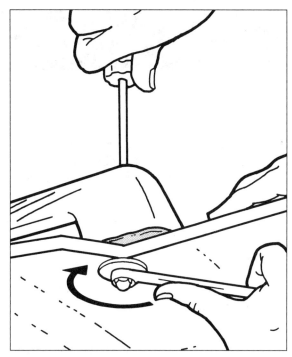

7 Wait until the sealant partially cures—30 minutes for silicone, 24 hours for polysulfide or polyurethane—then fully tighten the bolts by turning the nuts only to prevent breaking the seal around the shank of the bolt. If the fitting is attached with screws, withdraw them one at a time, run a bead of sealant around the shank beneath the head, reinstall each in turn, then drive them all home evenly.

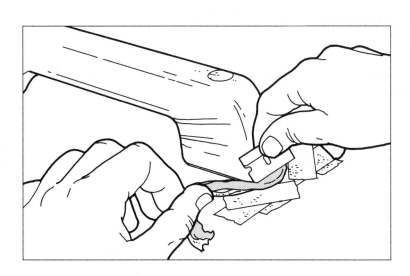

8 Trim away the excess squeeze-out by running a razor blade around the fitting, then peeling away the masking tape. Never leave a fillet around the edge; silicone attracts dirt, polyurethane yellows, and polysulfide weakens in the sun, so you want the least amount of sealant visible—only the thin edge beneath the fitting. Install new bungs, matching color and grain and setting them with varnish.

PREPARING A CORED DECK FOR NEW HARDWARE

As good as marine sealants are, you should never depend on them to keep water out of the core of a deck or hull. Anytime you drill or cut a hole in the deck, seal the exposed core with epoxy before mounting any hardware. If you are rebedding old hardware for the first time, be certain that the core has been properly sealed, or follow this procedure before reinstalling the fitting.

1 Drill all fastener holes oversize. A large hole—for a through-hull fitting, for example—doesn't need to be cut oversize.

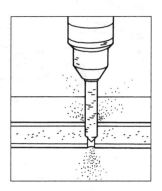

2 Remove all the core within ½ inch of the hole. You can do this easily with a bent nail chucked into a power drill. Vacuum the pulverized core from the cavity; whatever you can't remove will act as a filler.

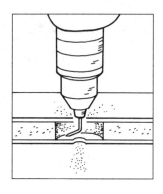

3 Fill the cavity with epoxy. The most secure way is a two-step process. First seal the bottom hole with duct tape, then pour catalyzed epoxy into the top hole. When the cavity is full, puncture the tape and let the epoxy run out back into your glue container. Filling the cavity with unthickened epoxy allows the epoxy to better penetrate the edge of the core. Retape the bottom hole. If there are several mounting holes, fill each and drain in turn until all have been treated and all bottom holes resealed.

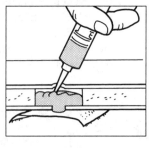

The second step is to thicken the epoxy (the same mix you have already poured through the holes) with colloidal silica to a mayonnaise consistency. Now fill each cavity level with the deck and allow the epoxy to cure fully.

4 Redrill the mounting holes through the cured epoxy. Sand and clean the area that will be under the fitting. Now you are ready to bed the new hardware as detailed in the previous section.

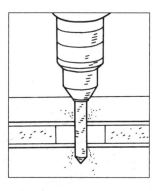

SEALING CHAINPLATES

When water finds its way below, very often the culprit is a leaking chainplate. Chainplates' propensity to leak is understandable; they are bedded under moderate fixed stress, but once under sail the windward chainplates are alternately yanked and eased while the leeward chainplates are virtually released. This tries the grip of any sealant. They are also stressed in unfair directions by poor sheet leads, shroud encounters with the dock, and by the use of shrouds for body support or as handholds for coming aboard. When the seal fails, rain and spray gathered by the attached shroud or stay runs down the wire and across the turnbuckle directly to the chainplate.

As annoying and potentially damaging as a leak into the cabin is, the larger risk is often from chainplates that appear to be watertight. The danger is usually not to the deck; most manufacturers know enough not to have chainplate openings located in a cored section of the deck (but you should check yours). It is the rig that is at risk. If the seal at the deck breaks, water penetrates, but additional sealant lower on the chainplate stops the leak before it enters the cabin. This results in the chainplate sitting in a ring of water. Despite the corrosion resistance of stainless steel, this situation will, over time, almost certainly result in chainplate failure. Because the erosion is hidden by the deck and/or sealant, the only way to detect this problem—short of catastrophic failure—is to pull the chainplate and examine it. If you have never fully examined your chainplates, or if it has been a few years, you are strongly urged to pull them before you rebed them.

1 Remove the trim plate if there is one. This can usually be taped up out of the way, but rebedding is much easier if you disconnect the shroud or stay by slackening the turnbuckle and pulling the pin. Disconnect only one shroud at a time. Before releasing a stay always set up a halyard to support the mast.

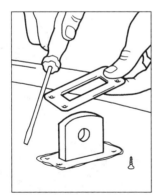

2 Pull the mounting bolts below deck and extract the chainplate. It is only necessary to remove the chainplate if you want to check it for signs of corrosion. If it doesn't come out easily, pass a long, round screwdriver shaft through the pinhole and support the end on a wooden block while lifting on the handle.

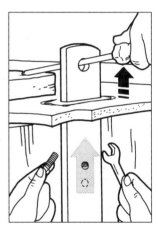

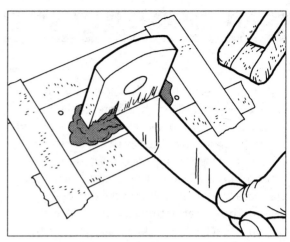

3 Dig all of the old caulk from the hole. A piece of hacksaw blade can be useful for this, but be careful not to enlarge the hole through the deck; the tighter the chainplate fits, the less it will move, and the longer your bedding job will last. Clean the deck, trim plate, and chainplate of old bedding. Examine the chainplate in the caulk area carefully; any pitting, cracks, or brown discoloration indicate replacement. Wipe down the deck, trim plate, chainplate, and the inside of the hole with acetone.

4 Reinstall the chainplate if you removed it. Dry-fit the trim plate and trace around it with a pencil. Mask the deck outside of the pencil line, the chainplate above the trim plate, and the top surface of the trim plate. Push a generous bead of polysulfide sealant into the space between the chainplate and the deck all the way around the chainplate. Use the flat of a flexible putty knife to force sealant into the crack. Butter the deck and the bottom of the trim plate with sealant.

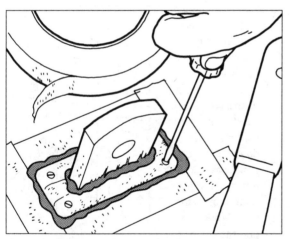

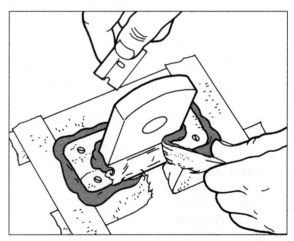

5 Fit the trim plate in position and install its fasteners. Because the trim plate screws are generally quite small, there is little to be gained by two-stage tightening, so tighten these screws fully. Sealant should squeeze out of the slot and all around the plate.

6 When the sealant is sufficiently cured, trace around the trim plate and the chainplate with a razor blade and remove the masking.

SEALING PORTHOLES—A TEMPORARY SOLUTION

When a porthole develops a leak, what you should do is rebed it properly. But maybe you're 500 miles offshore, and removing a porthole doesn't seem like a very good idea. Or maybe your end-of-season haulout is only three weeks away. Or maybe you just don't have the time or the inclination to get involved in such a job at the moment. You could just let the sucker leak, but a more sensible solution is a temporary repair.

1 Wipe the frame, cabin side, and portlight thoroughly with *alcohol* to remove any oil or grease. *Never use acetone or other strong solvents on plastic portlights or hatches.*

2 Mask both the portlight and the cabin side about ⅛ inch from the frame.

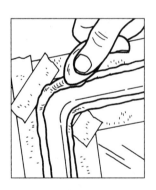

3 Push a thin bead of silicone sealant into the corners the frame forms with the portlight and with the cabin side. Drag a fingertip or a plastic spoon through the bead to form a concave fillet all the way around both edges of the frame.

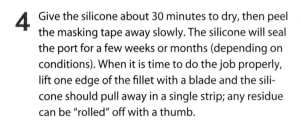

4 Give the silicone about 30 minutes to dry, then peel the masking tape away slowly. The silicone will seal the port for a few weeks or months (depending on conditions). When it is time to do the job properly, lift one edge of the fillet with a blade and the silicone should pull away in a single strip; any residue can be "rolled" off with a thumb.

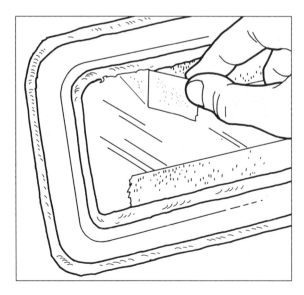

Opening portholes are rebedded like any other piece of hardware—by removing them, cleaning away all old caulk, buttering the cabin side and the outside flange with fresh sealant, snugging the fasteners, then tightening fully after the sealant has cured. Use polysulfide if the frames are metal, silicone (or a silicone hybrid) if they are plastic.

Getting a watertight seal around a fixed port is a bit more exacting.

1 Dismantle the deadlight. The deadlight pane is typically captured between inner and outer trim rings bolted together, either by through-bolts or by machine screws that thread into sockets on the outer ring.

NOTE: You may find a rubber gasket between the inner frame and the plastic pane. This is not a seal; it's a spacer. Boat manufacturers often installed acrylic windows thinner than the space between the trim rings, making up the difference with a rubber gasket. If you aren't replacing the pane, you will need this gasket. If it has hardened or deteriorated, cut a new one. Don't use soft gasket material; this will allow the pane to be pushed away from the outer frame, probably resulting in seal failure. Eliminating the gasket altogether by installing thicker portlights is the best plan (see next section).

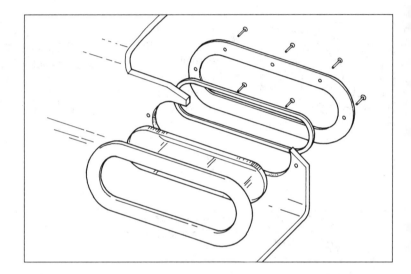

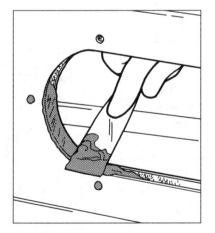

2 Remove all traces of old sealant and wipe all the surfaces with rubbing (isopropyl) alcohol. Check the edges of the cutout in the cabin side. If there is exposed core, dig it out beyond the screw holes and fill the cavity with epoxy thickened with colloidal silica. After the epoxy cures, redrill the fastener holes.

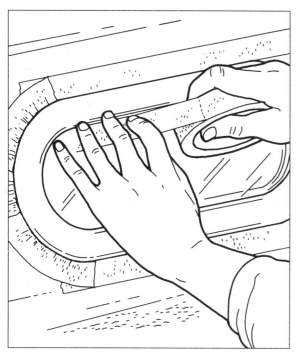

3 Reassemble the cleaned parts and mask both the portlight and the cabin side at the edge of the outer frame. Disassemble.

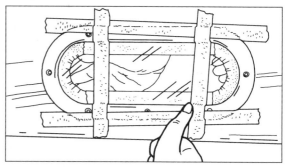

4 Tape the inside ring in place, then position the pane—with the gasket, if fitted—in position inside the cutout. A couple of strips of tape across the pane and frame inside the cabin will hold the pane in place.

5 Back up on deck, fill the space between the plastic and the cabin side with silicone-based adhesive sealant (Life Seal or equivalent). Continue applying sealant to the pane and cabin side until the unmasked edges of both are coated. Distribute the bedding with a putty knife.

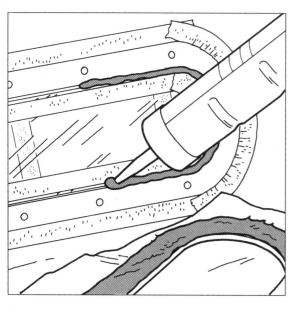

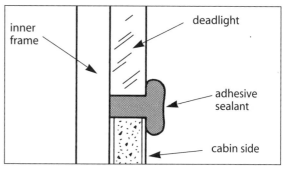

inner frame

deadlight

adhesive sealant

cabin side

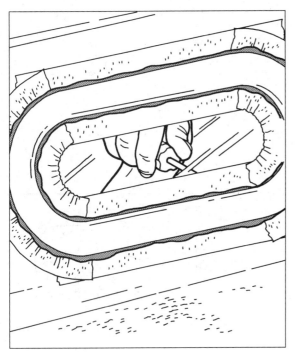

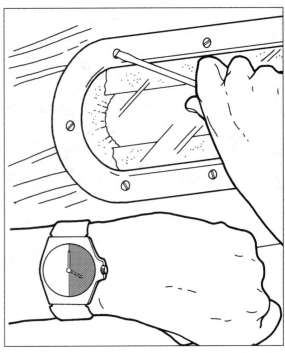

6 Butter the underside of the outside ring and install it. Snug the mounting bolts or machine screws until sealant squeezes from under every edge of the ring. If the rings are through-bolted, don't forget to put a bead of sealant under the head of each fastener.

7 Let the silicone cure for 30 minutes, then tighten the screws.

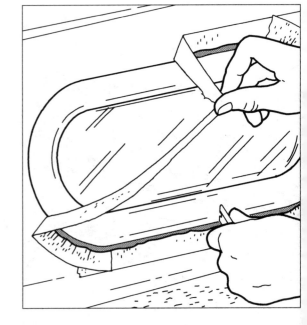

8 Run a new razor blade around both edges of the outside frame, then peel away the masking tape.

Old acrylic portlights get scratched, cloudy, and crazed, but because this happens gradually we often fail to notice until they are almost opaque. Replacing portlights is easy and inexpensive. You are sure to be amazed at the difference it will make in both the look of the boat and the clarity of the view.

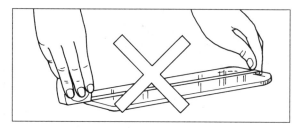

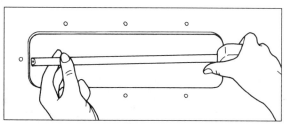

1 Measure the opening. Don't blindly copy the old pane. Mount the inner and outer frames without a pane and measure the space between them. This is the correct thickness for your new plastic—perhaps a few thousandths thinner to allow for expansion. Using a rubber gasket to fill the space is a poor compromise.

Also look at how the old portlight fits the opening. Often the corner radius of the opening and that of the pane are completely different, resulting in excessive gap at the corners. The new plastic should fit the opening (or the frame if it has a capturing flange) with an even gap of about $1/8$ inch all the way around. If the old pane isn't a good fit, cut a stiff paper pattern.

2 Take the measurements and patterns to the plastics supplier and have the pieces cut, or buy a sheet of plastic the proper thickness and cut them yourself. Both acrylic and polycarbonate can be cut and drilled with standard woodworking tools, but the edges must be well supported to prevent chipping. Special plastics blades will give the best results. Scrape away any slag with the back (smooth edge) of a hacksaw blade, then file or sand out any chips to eliminate any points that might lead to cracking. Leave the protective film on the plastic while fabricating and mounting.

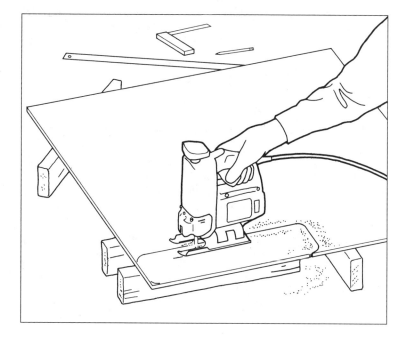

3 Dry-fit the new portlight and trace around the inside of both frames with the corner of a razor blade to cut the protective film. Dismantle the assembly and peel the film from the edges of the plastic.

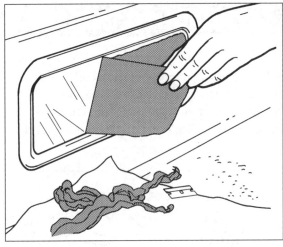

4 Bed the new pane as detailed in the previous section. When the sealant is cured, trace the frame with a blade and peel away the protective film.

ACRYLIC OR POLYCARBONATE?

WHEN CHOOSING THE MATERIAL FOR REPLACEMENT PORTLIGHTS, you have two choices. Acrylic—sold under such brand names as Plexiglas, Lucite, and Acrylite—is the plastic you are most likely to be replacing. Manufacturers use it because it is adequate and relatively cheap. Those may be good enough reasons for you to chose acrylic as well. Acrylic can be brittle and has historically exhibited a tendency to craze. Crazing is less of a problem with today's formulations, but stressed acrylic still cracks. However, for spans typical of boat portlights, acrylic of appropriate thickness is unlikely to break even in extreme conditions.

Polycarbonate—most familiar as Lexan—is not just a better acrylic. It is an entirely different thermoplastic and has an impact resistance roughly 20 times greater than acrylic. Polycarbonate's remarkable strength makes it the undisputed best choice for the wide spans of hatches and oversize windows, but it is probably overkill for most portlight installations. Polycarbonate is softer than acrylic and thus easier to scratch, and it tends to darken with age.

With the cost of polycarbonate about 2½ times that of acrylic, there is little reason to spend the extra money for polycarbonate portlights unless you are heading out to the high latitudes. Acrylic provides adequate strength for all but the most extreme conditions, is more scratch-resistant, and will remain bright longer. Of course if you would feel more secure with bulletproof portlights, that's what you should install.

Acrylics and polycarbonates are both available with coatings to make them more scuff-resistant, but in the marine environment these coatings invariably peel off like a bad sunburn. Opt for the less expensive basic untreated plastic; lost luster can be easily restored with a quality plastic polish.

Both plastics are easy to fabricate with common woodworking tools. Polycarbonate shows less tendency to chip, but more tendency to heat up in the cut and bind the blade. Lubricate the blade with beeswax or bar soap, and use a moderate blade speed.

DEAD FRAMES

THREADED SOCKETS, ESPECIALLY IN ALUMINUM frames, are prone to corrode and may strip when you back out the mounting screws. If that happens, you can still reuse the frames by drilling through the

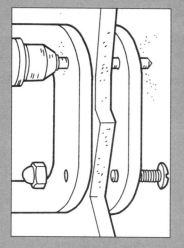

outside frame (down the center of the stripped sockets), countersinking the new holes, and through-bolting the frames with barrel screws or with oval-head screws and cap nuts.

Sometimes aluminum frames are so corroded underneath that they simply disintegrate when dismantled; if that happens, you can buy new frames from the original manufacturer, special order frames through Bomar, Vetus (W. H. Denouden), or Hood Yacht Systems, or have them fabricated by a local machine shop.

Deadlights are sometimes installed without a frame, captured in a rubber gasket like an old automobile windshield. The gasket may have a metal or plastic insert to "lock" it in position. Rubber-mounted deadlights are more often found on small boats and are probably safe enough for a boat used inshore. You work a new pane into the gasket with the aid of a soap solution and a rounded prying tool—like putting a tire on a rim—but by

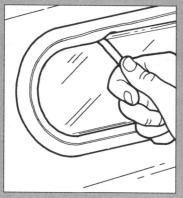

the time it is time to replace the pane, the rubber gasket is usually too brittle to stretch over the plastic without tearing. You may be able to find replacement gaskets, but if the boat will be operated outside of protected waters, where the punch of a boarding wave could push the portlight out of the gasket, consider reinstalling the pane with a rigid mounting system.

If you don't object to the change in look, one of the most secure methods of installing a deadlight is to simply cut the plastic pane an inch or so larger than the opening all around and

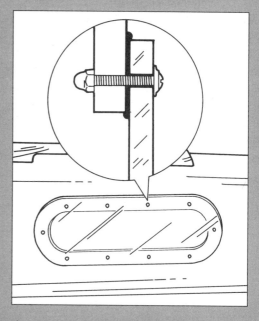

through-bolt the pane directly to the cabin side—well-bedded, of course. Drill the mounting holes a drill size or two oversize to allow the plastic to expand and contract. Space the holes at roughly 12 times the thickness of the pane. Don't countersink the holes; the wedge effect of countersunk fasteners will eventually crack the plastic. Instead, use panhead bolts (preferably with oversize heads) or use finishing washers under oval-head bolts. Hide the raw edges of the hole in the cabin side with trim.

MAST BOOTS

Leaks around a keel-stepped mast indicate boot failure. The time to install a new mast boot (or coat) is when the mast is being stepped. Universal molded replacement boots are available, but a cheaper, more versatile, and more durable alternative is a section of inner tube; your nearest tire dealer probably has a bin full of discards that would provide a suitable section.

Slip the boot up the mast inside out and upside down. Once the mast is stepped and the rubber chocks are in place, slide the boot down and clamp the lower end to the mast with a boot clamp (a BIG hose clamp). Now turn the top of the boot down over the clamp—like rolling down a sweatsock—and stretch it over the deck flange. A clamp around the flange completes the seal. If the mast has an extruded sailtrack, before installing the boot, fill the track in the clamp area with polysulfide sealant or epoxy putty and let the compound dry.

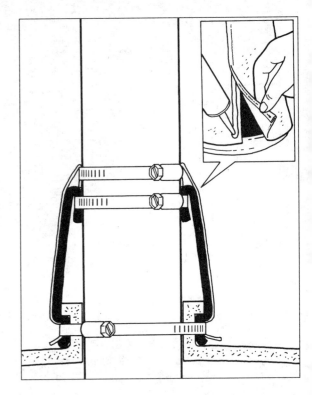

Extend the life of the boot by protecting it with a canvas coat. Cut the canvas so the edges overlap and "button" them with a bead of polyurethane after the coat is installed. The canvas should be captured under its own clamp on the mast, but it can share the flange clamp with the boot.

HULL-TO-DECK JOINT

In older fiberglass boats, deck joints are often an annoying source of leaks. Rare is the old fiberglass boat that doesn't exhibit a bead of silicone somewhere along the edge of the caprail or toerail, placed there in some past ill-fated attempt to stop the intrusion.

Better fastening techniques and better joint compounds have improved hull-to-deck joints, and these improvements can be applied to older boats.

EVALUATING THE JOINT

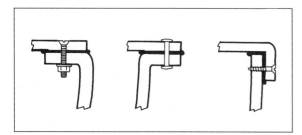

1 Most hull-to-deck joints fall into one of three categories: inboard flange, outboard flange, or shoebox. The best joints are fiberglassed together into a single strong and leak-free unit, but few boats are built this way. Most are joined mechanically with rivets, screws, or bolts, and depend on sealant to keep water out.

2 Gaining clear access to the deck joint almost always involves removing the rail, which requires bedding anyway. The outboard flange is generally the easiest joint to reseal. Cabin joinery can make access to the other types impossible without virtually dismantling the interior. In such cases, a compromise repair may be the best alternative.

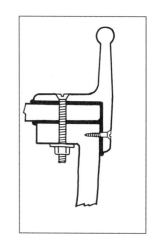

REBEDDING

How big the job of repairing a leaking hull-to-deck joint is depends almost entirely on how much dismantling is required to get to the joint fasteners. The good news is that if you do it right, you are unlikely to need to do it again for at least 20 years. Don't cut corners.

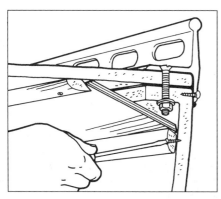

1 Remove the rail. Metal rails may be through-bolted (best), screwed in place (a distant second), or sometimes riveted (bad). Wood rails will be bolted or screwed; drill out the bungs to get at the heads of the fasteners. The nuts are often accessible behind easily removed panels in the cabin.

2 Remove mechanical fasteners holding the joint together. Don't be surprised if these are widely spaced; manufacturers often installed only a sufficient quantity to hold the flange together until the rail was installed, depending on the rail fasteners to do double duty. Grind the heads off any rivets and punch them out.

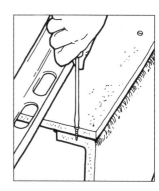

3 Reef out old bedding compound. Early fiberglass boats were bedded with an oil-based mastic that eventually dries out and shrinks. For a secure seal, all the old caulking must be removed. Clean the joint thoroughly with acetone, using a sharpened putty knife to separate the flanges as much as possible without damaging the laminate.

FIBERGLASSING

THE BEST SOLUTION FOR A LEAKING HULL-to-deck joint is to join the two parts permanently with fiberglass lay-up. This can be done either inside or outside, depending on access and the design of the joint. Instructions for laying up fiberglass are provided in "Laminate Repair."

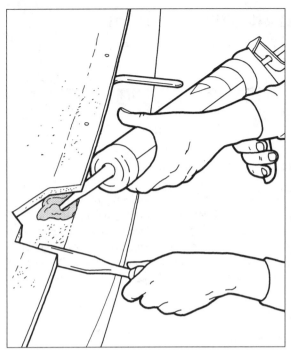

4 With the flange pried open, fill the gap with polyurethane sealant (3M-5200 or equivalent). For a permanent seal, it is imperative to have a continuous line of sealant that passes both outboard and inboard of the fastener holes.

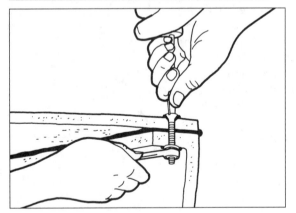

5 Refasten the flange. Through-bolt if possible. If not, use self-tapping screws, not rivets. Generously bed the bolts or screws in sealant.

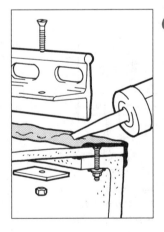

6 Reinstall the rail, bedding it as detailed earlier. Be sure to use backing plates or at least oversize shoulder washers under nuts holding slotted rail or T-track.

CENTERBOARD TRUNKS

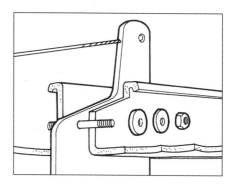

Wooden centerboard trunks are notorious leakers, but fiberglass trunks seldom leak except around the pivot pin. This is easily avoided by making the pin part of an internal frame that slips inside the case, but more often the pivot pin in a true centerboard boat—one without an external keel—passes through the trunk from inside the boat, sealed on either side by rubber grommets. When the grommets harden, a leak occurs. Tightening the nut is not the solution and may distort the case enough to jam the centerboard. Stop the leak by replacing the grommets.

Pulling the pivot pin with the boat afloat will admit a significant flow. This is a job better done with the boat out of the water. Be sure the centerboard is well supported when you pull the pivot pin or the board will drop out of the trunk.

In a keel/centerboard boat, the pivot pin usually passes through the stub keel. A leak here cannot be repaired effectively with grommets or sealant. Details for repairing the pivot pin of a keel/centerboard boat are provided in "Keel and Rudder Damage."

THROUGH-HULL FITTINGS

Through-hull fittings last a very long time, but occasionally require replacement. Modifications to the boat may necessitate an additional through-hull, but the prudent skipper will minimize the number of holes through the hull of his boat by tying into existing through-hulls whenever practical.

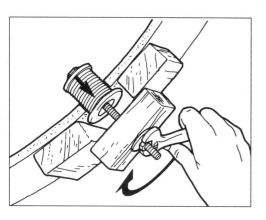

1 Removal of the old through-hull is easy with the aid of a long bolt and a washer large enough to sit on the through-hull. With the retaining nut or seacock removed, pass the bolt through the through-hull and through a wooden block outside the hull. Block the ends of the wood clear of the hull and tighten the nut on the bolt.

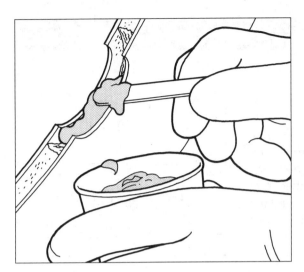

2 The hull must be solid around a through-hull. If the hull is cored, hollow an area around the hole at least as large as the flange of the seacock and fill the hollow with epoxy thickened to mayonnaise consistency with colloidal silica.

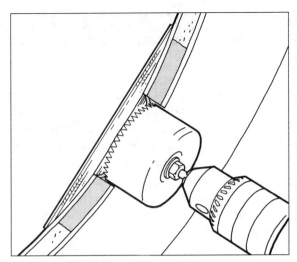

3 Fitting a flat seacock flange to the concave inner surface of a hull requires a contoured backer block. A backer block also spreads the load on the hull. The easiest backer block is a ring cut from plywood and shaped to the hull with a sander, but if you use plywood, saturate it with epoxy before you install it (cured), or the slightest seacock leak will quickly destroy it. Laminating incrementally larger circles of fiberglass to the hull to build up a flat island is a better approach (see "Laminate Repair" for laminating instructions). Capturing the flange bolts under the laminated pad to eliminate bolt holes through the hull makes a very nice installation. Drill the center hole in the pad (from outside) after the laminates cure.

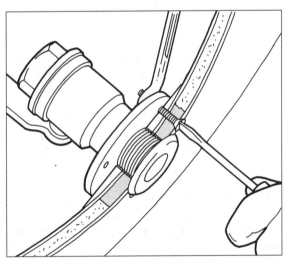

4 Assemble the through-hull and the seacock. If the through-hull bottoms out into the seacock, you need additional pad thickness. If you have not glassed in studs, drill and countersink mounting holes through the hull. Bolt the seacock in place; never install a seacock by simply threading it onto the through-hull. Bed the mounting bolts well.

5 Remove the through-hull, turning it with a file, steel plate, or hardwood wedge against the internal ears. Butter the hole, the edge, and the through-hull threads and flange with polyurethane sealant. Reinstall the through-hull and tighten; caulk should squeeze out all around the outside flange. Clean away the excess and use some of it to fair the heads of the flange bolts.

Some leaks into the cabin are obvious, but most aren't. Water may leak through the deck, then travel along the top of a headliner 10 feet or more before finding an exit and dripping out. The traditional way of finding leaks is to flood the deck, moving the hose incrementally "up" the deck until the drip appears. This method often fails. Here is a method that requires a bit more effort, but it will locate every leak.

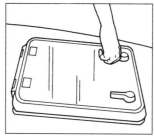

1 Shut all seacocks and close all hatches.

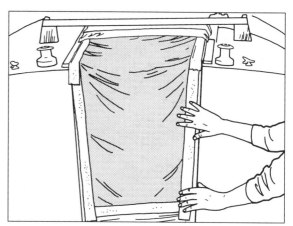

2 Use duct tape to seal all openings you don't expect to be airtight, i.e., ventilators, cockpit hatches, hawsepipes, etc. Seal the companionway with plastic sheeting (a garbage bag will be adequate) edge-taped over the hatch and the dropboards.

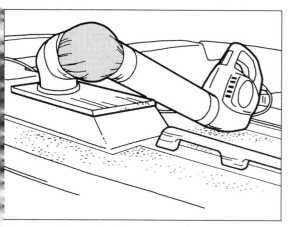

3 Insert the nozzle of a small electric leaf blower into an open ventilator or deck plate and seal it with tape. A shop-vac with the hose on the "blow" side will also serve.

With the blower running (give it five minutes to pressurize all the internal spaces), sponge soapy water over all ports, hatches, and hardware. Anywhere you see bubbles, you have a deck leak.

After you rebed the identified fitting, you can pressure-test again to confirm that the leak is

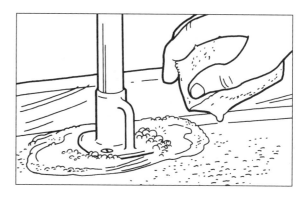

resolved, but don't leave the tape in place for more than a few hours—never overnight—or you will have great difficulty removing it.

RESTORING THE GLOSS

Production fiberglass boats are built by laying multiple laminates into a boat-shaped mold. The interior of the mold is polished mirror-bright and coated with a releasing agent (wax); then the first layer, called gelcoat, is sprayed onto the mold surface. The initial layer of fiberglass is applied to the "back" side of the gelcoat, and additional layers are added until the builder achieves the desired thickness.

This is opposite of the way most other products are manufactured, where the last step in production is to spray on the finish—presumably the reason it's called the finish. Gelcoat is the start.

Gelcoat also differs from paint in other important ways. The bond between paint and the underlying surface is mechanical—that Passion Fruit Crimson enamel on your old Roadmaster is hanging on (or not) by gripping microscopic scratches put there by sanding or chemically etching the metal. Between gelcoat and the underlying laminates, the bond is chemical; the resin saturating the first layer of glass material combines with the exposed surface of the gelcoat to form a single mass—not unlike pouring warm gelatin over cold. This is called chemical cross-linking, and it occurs because gelcoat resin and the polyester resin used to saturate the layers of fiberglass material are the same basic product. Gelcoat is essentially pigmented polyester resin.

Gelcoat resin has poor flow characteristics. Good paints are self-leveling—like water—drying to a smooth, glossy finish, but gelcoat resin behaves more like plaster, taking on the texture of the application tool. It can be thinned and sprayed to get a reasonably smooth finish, but the "wet-look" gloss characteristic of new fiberglass boats is due entirely to the highly polished interior surface of the mold.

Gelcoat is much thicker than a paint finish. For example, the dry film thickness (DFT) of a typical polyurethane finish (Awlgrip) is 1.5 to 2 mils (0.0015 to 0.002 inch) thick. The thickness of the gelcoat layer of a boat just popped from the mold is 20 mils, give or take 3 or 4 mils. In other words, the paint on a painted surface is typically thinner than a single page of this book, while a layer of gelcoat will normally be about 10 pages thick.

A well-applied gelcoat (like everything else, there are quality differences between manufacturers) will generally last 10 years with minimal or no care. Protected with an annual coat of wax and compounded in later years, gelcoat can maintain its gloss for 20 years or more. The longevity of gelcoat is due primarily to its thickness. When the surface dulls and chalks, the "dead" layer can be abraded off and the fresh surface underneath polished to restore the gloss.

Thickness can also be the enemy. If the builder applies the gelcoat too thickly—often done with the best intentions on early fiberglass boats—it eventually cracks like dried mud. A faulty resin formulation can also cause cracking and crazing.

Except for color matching, gelcoat repairs are easy and straightforward.

BUFFING

The most common surface malady of fiberglass boats is a dull finish. This is brought on almost entirely by exposure and can be delayed significantly by regularly waxing the gelcoat. When unprotected gelcoat becomes dull and porous, perhaps even chalky, waxing will no longer restore the gloss. The damaged surface must be removed by buffing the gelcoat with rubbing compound.

START WITH A CLEAN SURFACE

1 Wash. Scrub the surface thoroughly with a solution of 1 cup of detergent per gallon of water; choose a liquid detergent, such as Wisk. To make the solution even more effective, fortify it with trisodium phosphate (TSP), available at any hardware store. If the surface shows any signs of mildew, add a cup of chlorine bleach to the mix. Rinse the surface thoroughly and let it dry.

2 Degrease. Soap solutions may fail to remove oil or grease from the porous gelcoat. To degrease the surface, sweep it with an MEK-soaked rag. (Acetone can also be used, but the slower-evaporating MEK holds contaminants in suspension longer.) Protect your hands with rubber gloves and turn the rag often, changing it when a clean area is no longer available.

3 Dewax. Rubbing compound works like very fine sandpaper, and wax on the surface can cause uneven cutting. In addition, if the surface has silicone on it (nine boats out of ten do), the compound drags the silicone into the bottom of microscopic scratches, which will cause you grief if you ever paint the hull. Wipe the hull with rags soaked in toluene or a proprietary dewax solvent. Wipe in a single direction, usually diagonally downward toward the waterline.

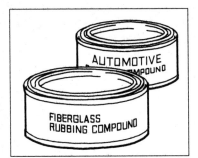

CHOOSE THE RIGHT COMPOUND

Gelcoat is much softer than paint and requires a gentler rubbing compound. Select a compound formulated for fiberglass. If the gelcoat is in especially bad shape, the heavier abrasion of an automotive compound can provide faster surface removal, but it must be used with caution to avoid cutting through.

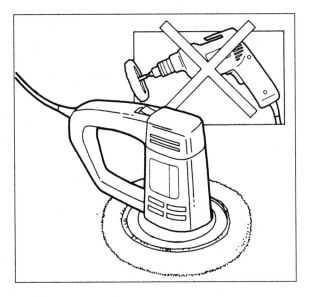

PLUG IN

Rubbing compound can be buffed out by hand if the area is small, but hand-buffing an entire boat is not recommended. An orbital polisher is far cheaper than an artificial elbow. Don't try chucking a buffing disk into your electric drill; it will eat right through the gelcoat, or you'll burn up the drill running it slow.

THE RIGHT PRESSURE

How much of the surface the compound removes relates directly to how much pressure you apply. Since you always want to remove as little gelcoat as necessary, never use any more pressure than is required. You will have to experiment with how much that is.

Whether you are compounding a small repair by hand or an entire hull with the aid of a machine, the process is the same. Working a small area at a time, apply the compound to the surface by hand, then buff it with a circular motion. Use heavier pressure initially, then progressively reduce the pressure until the surface becomes glassy.

If the gelcoat shows swirl marks, buff them out with a very fine finishing compound.

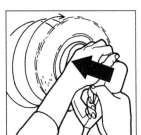

SANDING

Sometimes the dead layer of old gelcoat is so deep that removing it with rubbing compound becomes interminable. In that case, the process can be accelerated by sanding the surface first. This only works if the gelcoat is thick; if you sand through the gelcoat, it is too thin to restore and you will have to paint the surface to restore its gloss.

HIGH SPEED AND HIGH RISK

1 The safest way to sand gelcoat is by hand, but you can slash the time required to remove the dead surface layer by using a power sander. You will need a ¼-sheet finishing sander—called a palm sander. Load it with 120-grit aluminum-oxide paper (it's brown). It is a good idea to start in an inconspicuous spot to make sure your gelcoat is thick enough to take this treatment. Keep in mind that the sander is working at about 200 orbits per second, so keep it moving and don't sand any area more than a few seconds. Apply only as much pressure as needed to maintain contact. This first pass removes most of the material; if the gelcoat doesn't get transparent, good results from the remaining steps are likely.

2 Don't let the sander run over any high spots, ridges, or corners, or it will cut through the gelcoat regardless of how thick it is. Change paper when the amount of sanding dust diminishes.

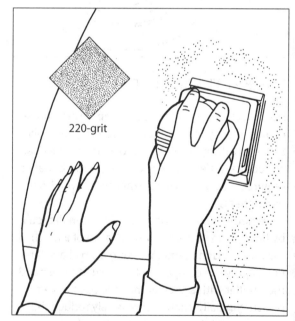

220-grit

3 When you have run the sander over the entire area, change to 220-grit paper and do it again.

WET SAND

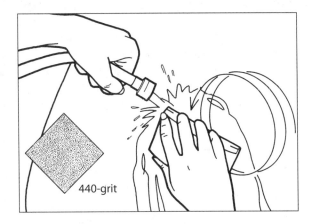

440-grit

1 Remove the scratch marks power sanding left behind by wet sanding the surface with 400-grit wet-or-dry (silicone carbide) sandpaper. Hand sand with a circular motion, keeping a trickle of water running on the sanding area.

2 To ensure a uniform surface, backing sandpaper with a rubber or wooden block is usually a good idea, but when the grit is very fine—320 or higher—you will get the same results and perhaps better control from finger-backed sanding. Fold the sandpaper as shown to keep the paper from sanding itself and to provide three fresh faces from each piece of paper.

3 Wear cloth garden gloves—the kind with the hard dots—to save the tips of your fingers.

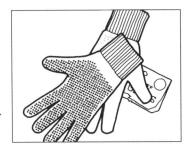

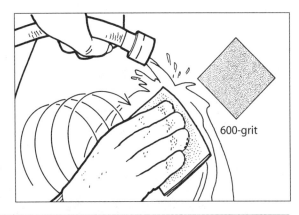

600-grit

4 Make a final pass with 600-grit wet-or-dry paper and the surface should be ready to buff to a like-new gloss.

WHAT?

THE HIGH SPEEDS OF PALM SANDERS—about 14,000 rpm—can result in an ear-damaging shriek. **Earplugs** are available from any drugstore for about a buck; buy a pair and use them. Not only will they save your hearing, but by eliminating the fatigue that accompanies such an assault on the senses, they actually make this job much easier.

SCRATCH REPAIR

Scratches are less visible on gelcoat than on paint since they don't cut through to some different color base. If the surrounding gelcoat is in good condition, always make surface damage repairs with gelcoat rather than paint. Even though the gelcoat application may initially be rough, it can be sanded smooth and polished to blend imperceptibly with the rest of the hull. For dealing with deeper gouges that also damage the underlying laminates, see "Hull Repairs."

OPENING A SCRATCH FOR REPAIR

Never try to repair a scratch by simply painting over it with gelcoat. Gelcoat resin is too thin to fill the scratch, and if the resin is thickened to a paste, the paste bridges the scratch rather than filling it. To get a permanent repair, draw the corner of a scraper or screwdriver down the scratch to open it and put a chamfer on both sides.

GELCOAT CHOICES

You will find gelcoat available as both a resin and in a thicker putty form called paste. Paste is what you want for scratch repair. Kits containing a small amount of gelcoat paste and hardener along with a selection of pigments can be purchased for less than $20.

WHAT COLOR IS WHITE?

THE HARDEST PART OF A REPAIR TO THE SURFACE of a fiberglass boat is matching the color. Even professionals that do gelcoat repairs daily have difficulty getting a perfect match. This is one of the few places that may call for conditioning yourself to be happy with a self-assessment of "not bad."

You can purchase gelcoat as unpigmented resin, in a kit with a half-dozen different colors of inorganic pigments, or in "factory" colors for the most popular boats. Because pigments fade, if a boat has seen a few years in the sun, even factory colors won't match exactly.

For small repairs to a white boat, a kit with pigments should serve; getting close is much easier with white, and once the repair is buffed out to a gloss, small shading differences will be unnoticeable.

For colored hulls and larger repairs, getting an adequate match is more difficult. It essentially requires tinting an ounce of gelcoat with one drop of pigment at a time and touching the resulting mix to the hull until you get a match. Keep track of the number of drops of each tint per ounce to reach the right color. Guys, get your wives or girlfriends to help you with this part; men are eight times more likely to have defective color vision—a minus that becomes a plus if your repair is slightly off (you won't notice).

For additional assistance in matching colors, see *Sailboat Refinishing* in this series.

CATALYZING

The hardener for gelcoat is the same as for any polyester resin—methyl ethyl ketone peroxide, or MEKP. Gelcoat resin usually requires 1 to 2 percent of hardener by volume (follow the manufacturer's instructions). As a general rule, four drops of hardener will catalyze 1 ounce of resin at 1 percent. The mix shouldn't kick (start to harden) in less than 30 minutes. Hardening in about two hours is probably ideal. *Always err on the side of too little hardener.* Also be certain to stir in the hardener thoroughly; if you fail to catalyze every bit of the resin, parts of the repair will be undercured.

SPREADING GELCOAT PASTE

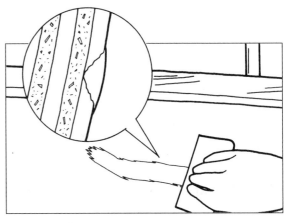

1 Original gelcoat is chemically bonded to the underlying laminates, but this molecular bond applies only to lay-up; the bond between a long-cured hull and an application of fresh gelcoat over a ding or scratch is strictly mechanical—just like paint. Wiping the scratch with styrene just prior to coating *can* partially reactivate the old gelcoat and result in some chemical crosslinking, but as a practical matter this step is usually omitted.

2 Apply gelcoat paste like any other putty; a plastic spreader works best. Let the putty bulge a little behind the spreader; polyester resin shrinks slightly as it cures, and you're going to sand the patch anyway. Just don't let it bulge too much or you'll make extra work for yourself.

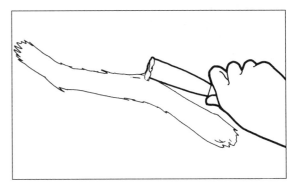

3 Scrape up any excess beyond the patch area.

COVERING THE REPAIR

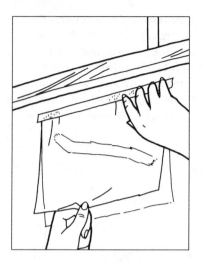  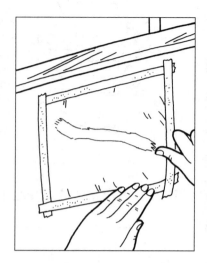

Gelcoat will not fully cure in air. Large repairs require a coating of polyvinyl alcohol (PVA) to seal the surface (see "Laminate Repair"), but to seal a scratch repair, cover it with a sheet of plastic. A section of kitchen "zipper" bag works especially well because it tends to remain smooth and the gelcoat will not adhere to it. Tape one edge of the plastic to the surface just beyond the repair, then smooth the plastic onto the gelcoat and tape down the remaining sides.

SANDING AND POLISHING GELCOAT REPAIRS

After 24 hours, peel away the plastic. The amount of sanding required will depend on how smoothly you applied the gelcoat.

1 For a scratch repair, a 5-inch length of 1 x 2 makes a convenient sanding block. Wrap the block with 120- or 150-grit paper, and use the narrow side to confine your sanding to the new gelcoat. Use short strokes, taking care that the paper is sanding only the patch and not the surrounding surface. Never do this initial sanding without a block backing the paper.

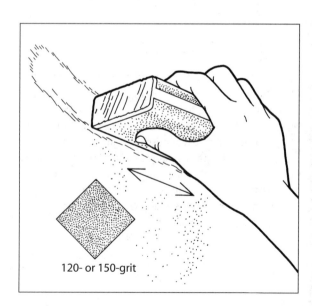

120- or 150-grit

2 When the new gelcoat is flush, put 220-grit wet-or-dry paper on your block and wet sand the repair, feathering it into the old gelcoat until you can detect no ridge with your fingertips.

3 Switch to 400-grit wet-or-dry, abandoning the block, and wet sand the surface until it has a uniform appearance. Follow this with 600-grit wet-or dry.

4 Dry the area and use rubbing compound to give the gelcoat a high gloss. On small repairs, you can buff the gelcoat up to a gloss by hand. Give the repair area a fresh coat of wax. If your color match is reasonably good, the repair will be virtually undetectable.

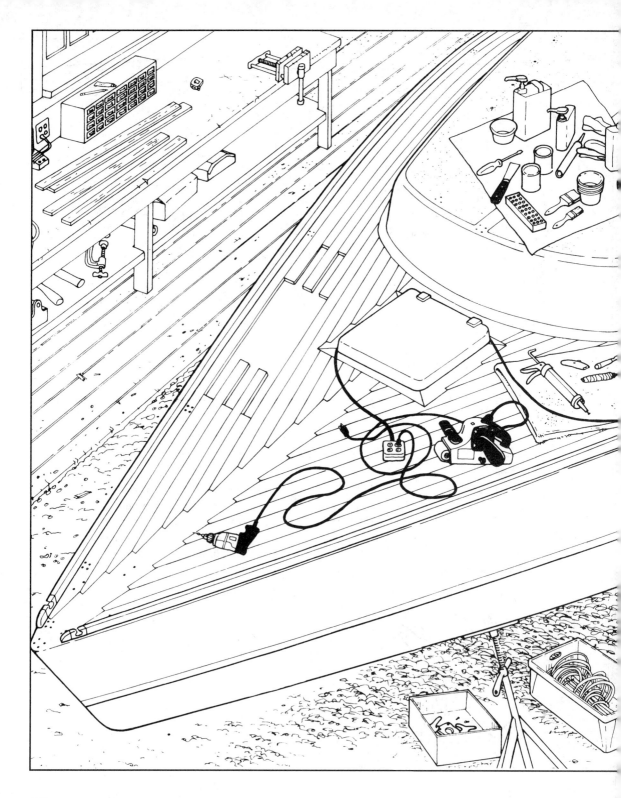

DECK REPAIRS

A fiberglass boat is typically molded in two sections: the hull and the deck. Most of the furniture and machinery is installed inside the open hull before the deck goes on—like filling a box before putting on the lid.

If you stay off the rocks and don't smash into the dock, the hull has a pretty good life—coddled by the water and always half in the shade. The deck, on the other hand, is born to a life of abuse. It sits out in the sun like a piece of Nevada desert. It is assaulted by rain, pollution, and foot. It is eviscerated by openings, pierced by hardware, pried by cleat and stanchion.

You might think that to stand up to such treatment, decks are as strongly built as the hull they cover. You'd be wrong. Weight carried low in a boat has little detrimental impact—a builder can make the hull as thick as he feels like—but weight carried high reduces stability. A deck must first be light; strength is defined by "strong enough." As a result, the need for deck repairs is far more common than the need for repairs to the hull.

Deck repairs can also be more complicated (but not necessarily "harder"). While the surface of a hull is flat or uniformly curved and relatively featureless, a deck is a landscape of corners, angles, curvatures, and textures. Damage often extends under deck-mounted hardware. Backside access may be inhibited by a molded headliner. And to provide stiffness without weight, deck construction generally involves a core.

In this chapter we will confine repairs to surface damage. This is hardly a constraint; most deck problems are limited to the deck's top surface.

RECOGNIZING STRESS CRACKS

Stress cracks are easy to identify by their shape. Typically the cracks run parallel or fan out in starburst pattern. You will see parallel cracks in molded corners, such as around the perimeter of the cockpit sole or where the deck intersects the cabin sides. These suggest weakness in the corner. Parallel cracks also show up on either side of bulkheads or other stiffening components attached to the inside surface of the hull or deck. The concentration of flexing stresses at such "hard spots" causes the gelcoat, and sometimes the underlying laminate, to crack.

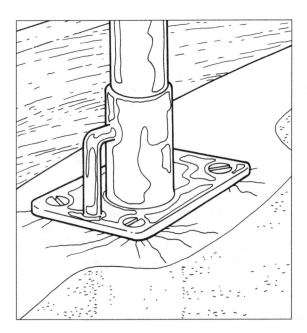

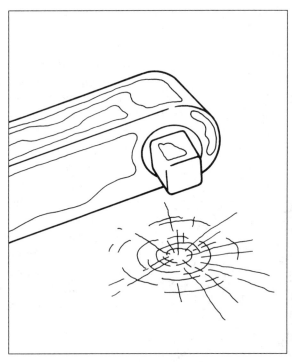

Starburst cracks are also caused by flexing, but in this case the movement centers at a point rather than along an edge. The most common starburst cracking extends from beneath stanchion mounts, brought about by falling against lifelines or by pulling oneself aboard with the top of the stanchion, which literally levers the deck up around the socket mounting holes.

Another cause of starburst cracking is point impact, such as dropping an anchor or a heavy winch handle on deck. (Exterior impact may instead result in concentric cracks—like the pattern of a target.)

ELIMINATING THE CAUSE

Backing plates.
Starburst cracking can usually be stopped by installing generous backing plates on the underside of the deck beneath the offending hardware to spread the load. Wooden plates are the easiest to fabricate, but stainless steel or bronze are better because of their resistance to crushing. Bevel the edges of the backing plate to avoid causing a hard spot. Polished stainless steel plates with threaded holes make for an attractive installation.

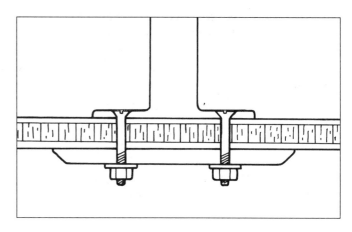

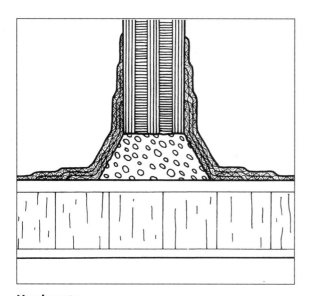

Hard spots.
Hard spots are more common on the hull than the deck, and usually appear where bulkheads attach. Stress cracks around hard spots are likely to return unless you eliminate the hard spot. This typically involves detaching the offending fixture, shaving some material from the edge, then reattaching it mounted on a foam spacer. Realistically, the work required may exceed the benefit, but anytime a bulkhead is detached or a new bulkhead is installed, it should always be mounted with a foam spacer.

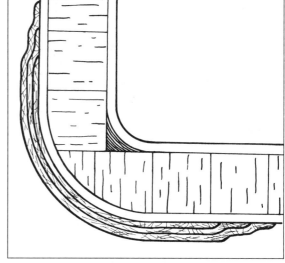

Stiffening.
Stress cracks related to general laminate weakness, such as those that too often appear around cockpit soles, can be prevented by stiffening the area with additional laminates. Laminating instructions are provided in "Laminate Repair." In this case you are trying to add stiffness, not strength, which translates into laminate thickness; use fiberglass mat to quickly build additional thickness.

REPAIRING THE CRACKS

Cracks in the deck typically affect only the gelcoat layer, and perhaps the first layer of mat beneath the gelcoat. Repairs are identical to scratch repair detailed in the previous chapter, except that you may need to remove deck hardware to get full access to the damage. Occasionally flexing has been so severe that stress cracks extend into the woven fabric of the laminate. When this is the case, the strength of the laminate is compromised, and the area must be ground out and relaminated to restore it. Detailed instructions for this type of repair are found in "Hull Repairs."

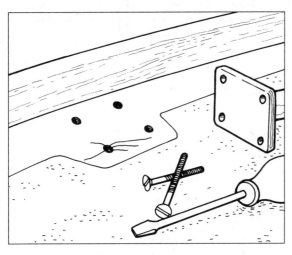

1 Gain access to the entire length of the crack.

2 Open the crack with the corner of a cabinet scraper.

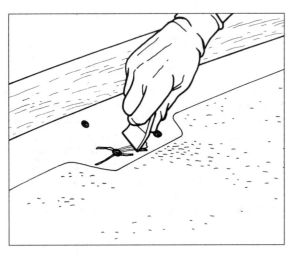

3 Fill it with gelcoat paste.

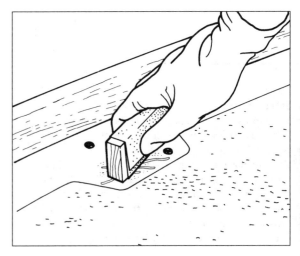

4 Sand and buff.

VOIDS

Voids are thankfully rare in the flat expanses of hull lay-up, but all too common in fiberglass decks. Voids occur when the first layer of cloth is not compressed against the gelcoat (or when a subsequent laminate is not compressed against the previous one). They are often as much a consequence of design as of workmanship. While crisp angles and corners may look stylish, they are more difficult to mold with glass fabric. The fabric resists being forced into a tight corner and after saturation may take a more natural shape, pulling away from the gelcoated mold. The result is a void—a pocket of air beneath the thin gelcoat, perhaps "bird caged" with a few random strands of glass. The first time pressure is applied, the gelcoat breaks away like an eggshell, revealing the crater beneath.

Deck voids are a cosmetic problem and easily repaired.

1 Break away the cracked gelcoat to fully expose the void.

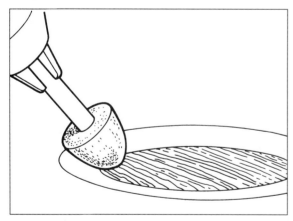

2 Use a rotary grinding point chucked in your drill to grind the interior surface of the cavity. Chamfer the gelcoat all around the void.

3 Clean the cavity with acetone. For a better bond, wipe the cavity with styrene.

4 Fill the cavity to the bottom of the gelcoat with a putty made from polyester resin and chopped glass. Be sure you use laminating resin, not finishing resin. Epoxy is not recommended because you are going to finish the repair with a layer of gelcoat, and gelcoat does not adhere as well to epoxy as to polyester.

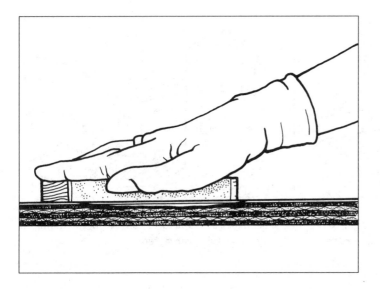

5 When the patch hardens, fill the remaining depression with gelcoat, overfilling slightly. Roll a piece of plastic into the repair and seal the edges with tape.

6 When the gelcoat cures, sand it flush with the surrounding surface and buff it with rubbing compound to restore the gloss.

CRAZING (ALLIGATORING)

Crazing, sometimes called alligatoring, is a random pattern of cracks that, at its worst, can cover the entire surface of a fiberglass boat—both deck and hull. There are two primary causes: flexing and excessively thick gelcoat. If flexing is the culprit, the crazing will be localized. For a repair to be successful, stiffening must be added to the deck in the area where the crazing has occurred.

Fortunately the more common cause of crazing is gelcoat thickness (or occasionally gelcoat formulation). As the hull heats and cools, it expands and contracts. A thin layer of gelcoat accommodates these changes, but thick gelcoat, not reinforced like the underlying laminates, tends to crack. In this case, the crazing is likely to be extensive. That's the bad news; the good news is that the repair doesn't require any structural alterations.

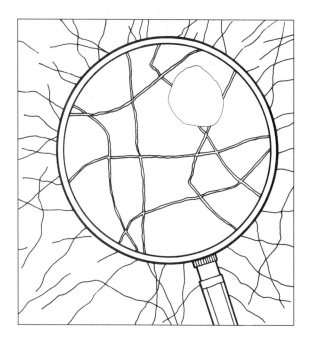

LOCALIZED CRAZING

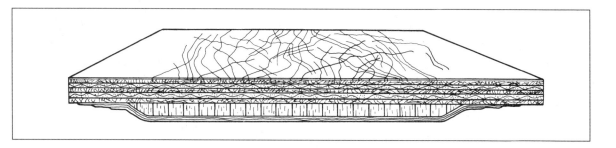

1 Stiffen the crazed area. See "Core Problems" for alternatives and step-by-step instructions.

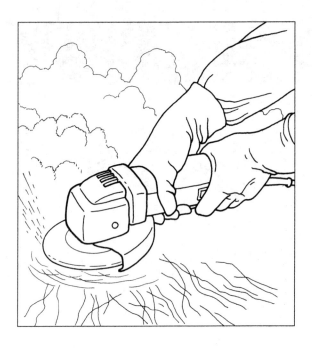

2 Trace each crack with the corner of a cabinet scraper, or if the pattern is too fine, grind the area with a 36-grit sanding disk. Stop when the disk begins to break through the gelcoat; don't grind all the gelcoat away.

3 Paint the cracks or ground area with color-matched gelcoat paste. Seal the surface to let the gelcoat cure.

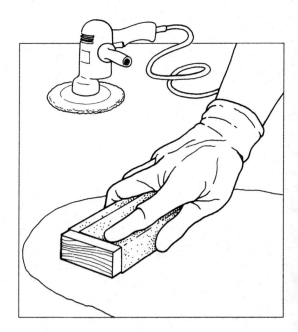

4 Fair the new gelcoat by block-sanding, then buff to a gloss.

WIDESPREAD CRAZING

Sanding and polishing surface-applied gelcoat is worthwhile when the new gelcoat area is relatively small and the rest of the gelcoat is in good condition, but when the majority of the original gelcoat is damaged, the labor intensive nature of gelcoat application suggests a different approach. The best alternative is painting the entire deck with a two-part polyurethane paint.

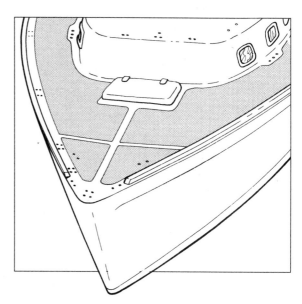

1 Remove as much deck hardware and trim as possible. The quality of your refinishing job is directly related to how much hardware you remove—how unobstructed the deck is when you apply the paint.

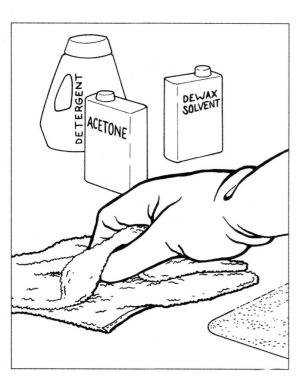

2 Clean, degrease, and dewax all the smooth surfaces of the deck. (Nonskid surfaces are restored in a separate process.)

3 Sand the gelcoat thoroughly with 120-grit sandpaper and wipe it dust-free with solvent.

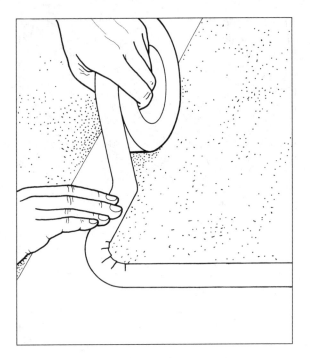

4 Mask nonskid surfaces and any hardware you have elected not to remove.

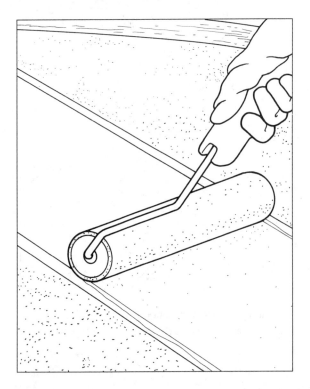

5 Paint the sanded gelcoat with a high-build epoxy primer. Apply the primer with a foam roller. Two coats are generally necessary to fill all crazing and porosity; machine sand each coat with 120-grit paper.

6 Paint the primed surfaces with two coats of two-part polyurethane, following the manufacturer's instructions for rolling and/or brushing the paint. For complete instructions on repainting decks—and all other boat surfaces—see *Sailboat Refinishing* in this book series.

RENEWING NONSKID

If you paint the smooth surfaces of the deck, you will probably want to refinish the nonskid surfaces as well. Painting nonskid surfaces tends to reduce their effectiveness. You can easily offset this by adding grit to the paint.

Always refinish the textured sections of the deck after the smooth portion. There are two reasons for this order. First, the nonskid surface is almost always a darker color than the smooth surfaces, and it is easier to cover a lighter color with a darker one than the other way around. Second, if the final masking is done on the textured surface, it will be hard to get a sharp line between the two. Prepare textured surfaces for refinishing before painting the other parts of the deck.

ENCAPSULATED GRIT

1 Scrub the nonskid thoroughly with a stiff brush, then use terry cloth—sections of old bath towels—to dewax the surface. The rough surface of the terry cloth penetrates the craggy nonskid.

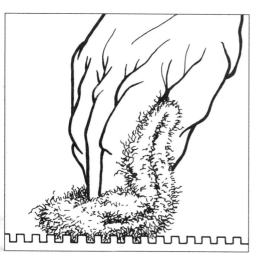

2 You can't sand the bottom surfaces of the nonskid, but abrade it with coarse bronze wool, using short, quick strokes. Fortunately most of the stress on the new paint will be on the top surface, which you can sand with 120-grit paper. Flood the surface and brush-scrub it again, then let it dry.

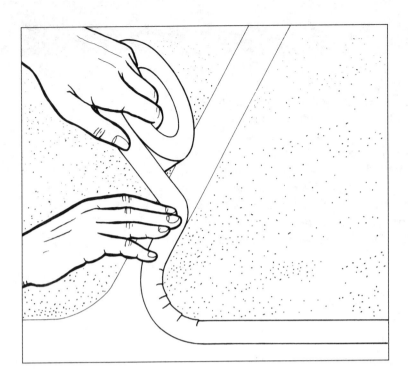

3 After the smooth surfaces are painted and dry, mask them at the mold line of the nonskid.

4 Mix a nonskid paint additive into the paint and roll it on with a medium-nap roller. (There is never any reason to "tip out" the paint on a nonskid surface.) This is the easy way to introduce grit into the paint, but because the additive—usually polymer beads—tends to settle to the bottom of the paint tray, dispersion of the grit on the painted surface can be irregular.

For a more aesthetically pleasing result, first coat the nonskid area with an epoxy primer and cover the wet epoxy with grit sifted from your fingers or a large shaker. When the epoxy kicks, gently sweep off the grit that didn't adhere (you can use it on another nonskid area), and encapsulate the grit that remains with two rolled-on coats of paint.

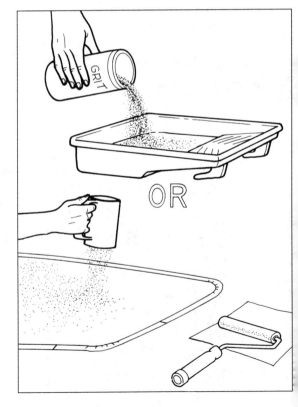

RUBBERIZED OVERLAY

For the best footing, you may want to consider a rubberized nonskid overlay, such as Treadmaster M or Vetus deck covering, also good choices for completely hiding old, worn-out nonskid textures. For overlay application, carry the paint ½ inch into the nonskid area when you paint the deck.

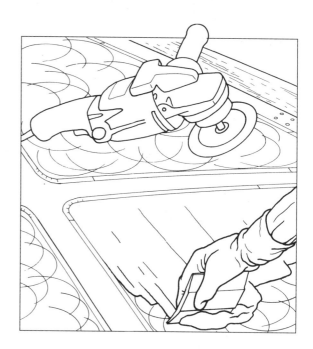

Preparing the surface.
Eliminate all molded texture. Most of it can be quickly taken off with a disk sander and a 36-grit disk. (A belt sander can also be used.) Be careful not to let the sander get outside the textured area. It is neither necessary nor desirable to *grind* away all the pattern. *Fill* the remaining depressions with epoxy putty. When the epoxy cures, sand the surface to fair it and prepare it for the adhesive.

Cutting patterns.

1 Make a pattern from kraft paper for each of the nonskid panels. Cut the paper oversize, then place it on deck to trace the exact outline. Tape across holes cut in the center of the paper to hold it in place. Use a flexible batten to draw curved edges, a can lid for uniform corners. For appearance and drainage, leave at least 1 inch between adjacent panels, at least twice that between the nonskid and rails, coamings, or cabin sides. Write "TOP" on the pattern to avoid confusion when you cut the overlay, and draw a line on it parallel to the centerline of the boat, with an arrow toward the bow.

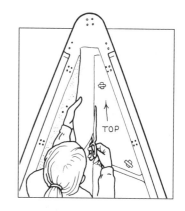

2 Do not cut patterns for only one side, expecting to reverse them for the opposite panels. Boats are almost never symmetrical, and hardware is certain to be in different locations. Cut a separate pattern for every panel. When all the patterns have been cut, tape them all in place and evaluate the overall effect before proceeding. Trace around each pattern with a pencil to outline the deck area to be coated with adhesive.

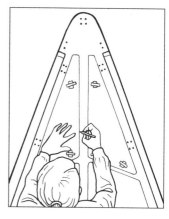

Cutting the overlay.

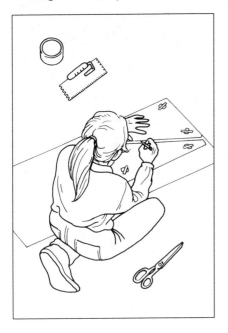

1 Place the patterns topside down on the back of the overlay material. Position all the patterns on your material to minimize the waste before making any cuts. Depending on the overlay you have chosen, it may be necessary to align the patterns; use the line you drew on each pattern for this purpose, aligning it parallel to the long edge of the sheet of material. Trace each pattern onto the overlay.

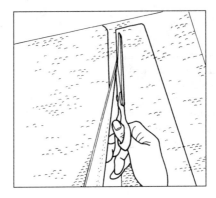

2 Cut out the pieces with tin snips or heavy scissors.

Applying the overlay.

1 If the overlay manufacturer doesn't specify a different adhesive, glue the nonskid to the deck with thickened epoxy. Coat both the outlined deck area and the back of the nonskid with the adhesive, using a serrated trowel.

2 Position the nonskid on the deck and press it flat, beginning with pressure in the middle and working outward to all edges.

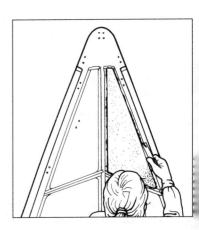

3 Pick up any squeeze-out with a putty knife, and clean away the residue with an acetone-dampened cloth. Continue applying each section in turn until all are installed.

CLEANING

Left untreated, good-quality teak would normally weather to an attractive ash gray, but the assault of modern-day air pollutants turns bare teak nearly black. Clean it with the mildest cleaner that does the job. Start with a 75/25 mixture of liquid detergent and chlorine bleach (no water), boosted with TSP. Apply this with a stiff brush, scrubbing lightly with the grain. Leave the mixture on the wood for several minutes to give the detergent time to suspend the dirt, and the bleach time to lighten the wood, then rinse thoroughly by flooding and brushing.

LIGHTENING

As good as chlorine is at bleaching cotton sweat-socks, it's not a very effective wood bleach. For that you need oxalic acid. You can get it by buying a commercial single-part teak cleaner—oxalic acid is the active ingredient in most—or for about one-tenth the price you can buy a can of Ajax household scouring powder. Whichever you select, brush the cleaner onto wet teak and give it time to work, then scrub the wood with Scotchbrite or bronze wool. (Never, ever, ever use steel wool aboard your boat—it will leave a trail of rust freckles that will be impossible to remove.) Oxalic acid dulls paint and fiberglass, so wet down surrounding surfaces before you start, and keep them free of the cleaner. Rinse the scrubbed wood thoroughly; brushing is essential.

For potential treatments for teak decks, see *Boat Refinishing* in this series.

TWO-PART CLEANERS

Two-part teak cleaners are dramatically effective at restoring the color to soiled, stained, and neglected teak, but these formulations contain a strong acid—usually hydrochloric—and should only be used when all other cleaning methods have failed.

1 Wet the wood to be cleaned, then use a *nylon-bristle brush* to paint part 1 onto the wet wood, avoiding contact with adjoining surfaces. If you use a natural-bristle brush, the cleaner will dissolve the bristles; it is doing the same thing to your teak.

2 Scrub with the grain.

3 Part 2 neutralizes the acid in part 1 and usually has some cleaning properties. Paint sufficient part 2 onto the teak to get a uniform color change. Scrub lightly.

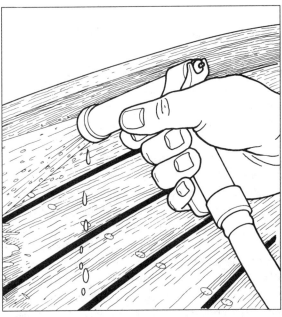

4 Flush away *all* traces of the cleaner and let the wood dry.

SURFACING

After a number of years, bare teak decks become rough and ridged. This unevenness traps dirt and harbors mildew, making the deck harder to clean and harder to keep clean. The solution is to resand the deck with a belt sander, using a 120-grit belt. Keep the sander moving at all times, and sand at about 15° to the grain.

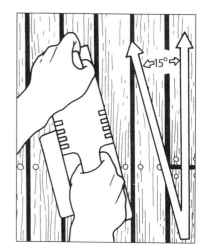

RECAULKING

The instructions that follow are for recaulking a section of a single seam, but the steps are the same for an entire deck.

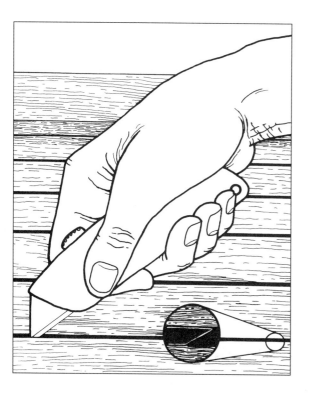

1 With a razor knife, cut the seam caulk at a diagonal a couple of inches beyond the bad section, then slice the section to be replaced free from the planks on either side, taking care not to nick the wood.

2 Dig out the old caulk. This is much easier with a rake made by heating the tail of a file and bending it about 90°. When every bit of the old caulk is off the planks, vacuum the scrapings out of the seam.

3 Use an acid brush or a Q-Tip to thoroughly prime both plank edges. Use the primer recommended for the caulk you are using. Two coats are generally required.

4 Mask the surface of the planks.

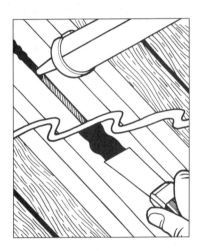

5 The "right" caulk for deck seams is two-part polysulfide. Mix the catalyst into the sealant per label instructions, taking care not to introduce bubbles, then fill an empty caulk tube with the mixture. (For limited repairs, a single-part polysulfide will also give good results and may be more convenient.) Cut the tip of the tube and fill the seam from the bottom. When the entire seam is slightly overfilled with sealant, compress it into the seam by dragging a putty knife over it firmly. The sealant will hump up slightly behind the knife, but it will shrink almost flush as it cures. Remove the masking carefully while the caulk is still tacky.

IDENTIFYING DECK CAULKING FAILURE

HOW DO YOU KNOW WHEN THE SEAM caulking on a teak deck has released its grip on the wood? The wood usually tells you. On a sunny day, scrub the deck, then keep it wet for half an hour or so before letting it dry. Areas along the seams that stay wet longer than the rest of the deck are suspect; spots that stay dark a lot longer definitely indicate caulk failure. Using the point of a knife, you will see that you can separate the caulk from the wood, and the edge of the plank will be wet. Repair all "flagged" seams before they result in bigger problems beneath the teak.

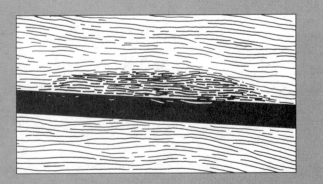

BUNG REPLACEMENT

The most common problem of teak decks is popped bungs. Years of scrubbing thins already-thin overlay planks until the grip of the bungs is insufficient to hold against flexing or expansion.

Just tapping a new bung in place will be a temporary repair at best. Deck overlay bungs require special procedures.

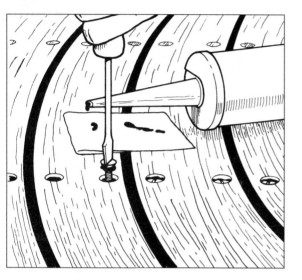

1 Remove and rebed the screw in polysulfide. Deck core problems often occur beneath teak overlay because the screws holding the overlay penetrate the top skin of the deck. *Always* rebed exposed screws. It is a good idea to check the core for sponginess with a piece of wire. (See "Core Problems.")

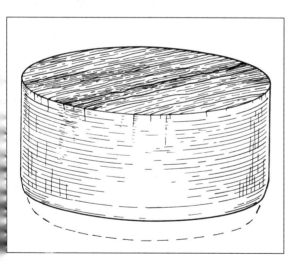

2 Reduce the plug bevel. In a shallow hole, you cannot afford the generous bevel found on most commercial teak plugs; sand the bottom of the plug to reduce it to the bare minimum.

3 Use a Q-Tip to wipe both the hole and the plug with acetone to remove surface oils. Wait 20 minutes to install the plug.

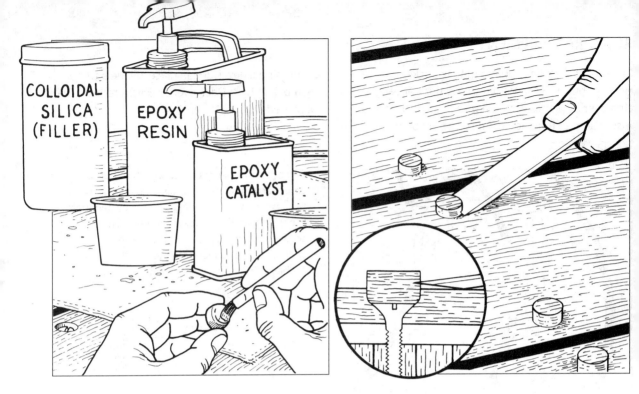

4 Mounting a plug permanently in a shallow hole requires the tenacious grip of epoxy glue. Paint the hole and sides of the bung with unthickened epoxy. Thicken the epoxy to catsup consistency with filler (colloidal silica) and coat the sides of the hole and plug. Tap the coated plug into the hole as far as it will go. Wipe up the excess glue.

5 After the epoxy is dry, place the point of a chisel—beveled side down—against the plug about $\frac{1}{8}$ inch above the surface of the plank and tap the chisel with a mallet. The top of the plug will split away.

6 Working from the lowest edge of the trimmed plug, pare away the plug until it is nearly flush with the plank. Finish the job by block sanding the plug with 120-grit sandpaper.

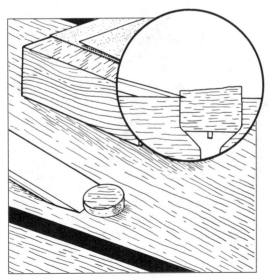

PLANK REPLACEMENT

Occasionally a teak plank splits or is otherwise damaged and requires replacement. More often teak overlay problems have an underlying cause—usually a wet core—and to effect repair the teak must be removed. Since the cause of the leakage often turns out to be the screw holes, some boat-owners elect not to replace the overlay, but most are unwilling to give up the beauty and footing of teak decks. A careful installation minimizes the risk to the core.

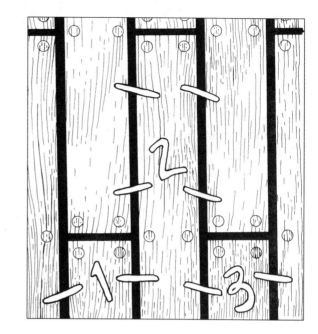

1 If you are replacing more than a single plank, number and crosshatch all the planks to be removed so you can put them back properly.

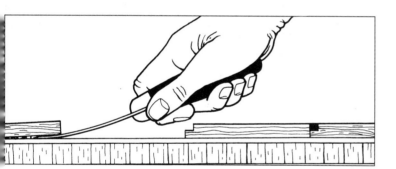

2 With bungs removed (carefully if you will be reusing the plank), extract the screws. Slice the plank free of the caulking all around, and pry the plank up from the bedding compound, using a block under your prying tool to protect the adjacent plank. If the plank is bedded in an organic compound, it should slowly pull free—like a gum-stuck heel. If it is bedded in polysulfide, you are likely to have to destroy the first plank to remove it. With side access, you should be able to separate the rest of the planks from the deck with a thin, sharpened putty knife. A length of steel leader wire connected to two lengths of dowel is sometimes effective in "cutting" deck planks free.

3 Scrape and sand away all old bedding compound.

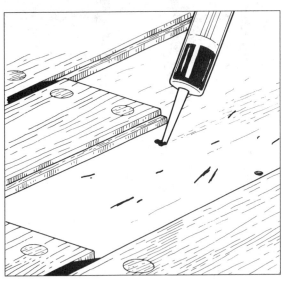

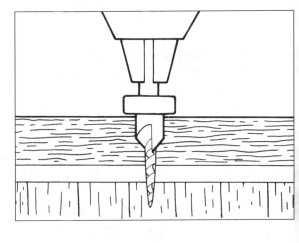

4 If the core is dry, protect it by injecting the hole full of epoxy. Give the epoxy a few minutes to saturate the edge of the core, then draw out the excess with a small brush or a stick. For greater security, drill each hole oversize and, after painting the sides with unthickened epoxy, fill each hole with epoxy thickened with colloidal silica. When the filler hardens, redrill the center for the screw.

5 If you are installing new planks, fill the old screw holes with epoxy putty, but don't redrill them. Wedge the new plank into position, then drill the plank and the deck. Counterbore the hole in the plank at least half the plank's thickness but not more than two-thirds. Epoxy the new holes in the deck in one of the two methods just detailed.

6 Wash the deck and the underside of the plank with acetone. For better adhesion, prime the teak. Coat the deck with black polysulfide (two-part preferred) and distribute it evenly with a saw-toothed spreader.

7 Hold or wedge the plank in position and screw it down. Select Philips-head screws and you will be much less likely to damage the edge of the bung hole with the screwdriver.

8 Install bungs (with epoxy) and trim them. Caulk the seams. Belt sand the deck fair.

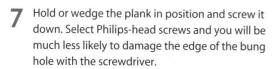

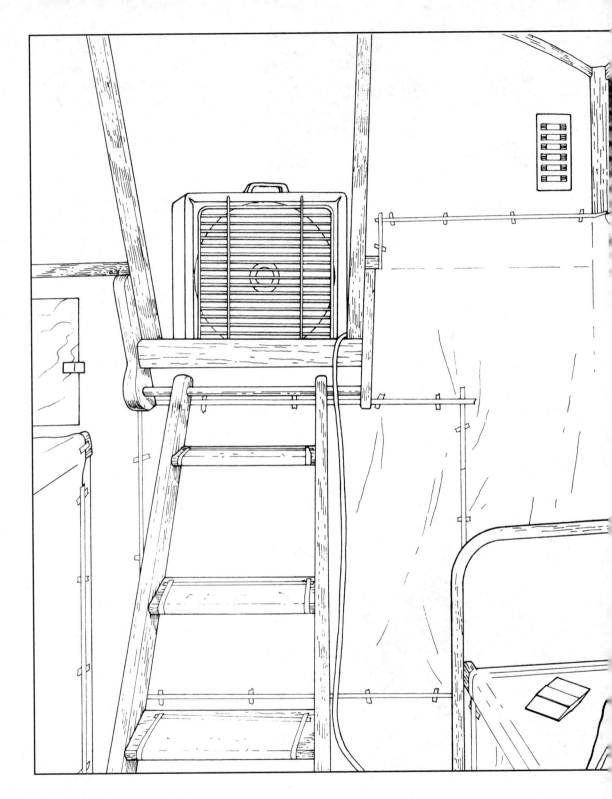

LAMINATE REPAIR

The hull and deck repairs described so far have either been cosmetic or leak related—problems that can be fixed with a proper topical application of one glop or another. But sometimes the problem is below the surface: the original laminate lacks the requisite stiffness; moisture has caused disintegration or delamination; or the glass fibers have been broken by impact. These problems require more extensive repair.

Fiberglass has become the predominant boatbuilding material because of its durability, but it is repairability that accounts for the near immortality of fiberglass boats. The most horrifying hole in a fiberglass hull is quickly healed with a bit of glass fabric, a can of resin, and equal parts skill and care. And the repair is less patch than graft—a new piece of skin indistinguishable from the old.

Fiberglass lay-up can hardly be simpler. It is nothing more than layers of glass fabric saturated with polyester (or epoxy) resin. With a paint brush, a cup of water, and a piece of old T- shirt, you can practice all the requisite skills for fiberglass lay-up.

Don't misunderstand: because of blocked access or complex shape, laminate repair cannot always be honestly characterized as easy, but such problems aren't what make most boatowners shy away from attempting a repair. It's the lay-up. Most boatowners imagine a self-applied laminate as only slightly more durable than a wet Band-Aid. That is a false concern. Follow a few simple rules—provided in this chapter—and your lay-up will be as good as or better than what you can expect a yard to do. And it will remain that way a decade down the road.

UNDERSTANDING POLYESTER RESIN

Polyester resin is the glue that binds glass fibers into the hard substance we call fiberglass. On the other side of the Atlantic, the same product is called GRP—glass-reinforced plastic. As usual, the British take more care with the language than we do; glass-reinforced plastic is *exactly* what it is.

Polyester resin, when catalyzed, hardens into plastic—not one of those tough plastics that deflects bullets or that you can use as a hinge for 100 years—but an amber-colored, rather brittle plastic that seems more like rock candy than boatbuilding material. But when polyester resin is combined with glass fibers, the sum is greater than the parts.

Polyester resins come in various formulations (see sidebar), although you can't always tell what kind a particular brand is from the label. Generally, you don't need to know. When polyester is appropriate for the repair (sometimes epoxy resin is a better choice), whatever laminating resin your supplier carries should prove satisfactory. Below-the-waterline repairs are the exception; avoid ortho resins if the repair will be continuously immersed.

LAMINATING VERSUS FINISHING

1 You do need to choose between laminating and finishing resin. Laminating resin is "air-inhibited," meaning that the resin will not fully cure while exposed to air. That may sound odd, but remember that polyester solidifies not by drying, like paint, but by a chemical reaction (called cross-linking) induced by adding a catalyst. Air interferes with this curing process.

For any job that requires the laminates to be applied in more than one operation, you need laminating resin. The fact that the surface remains tacky after the resin sets allows you to apply the subsequent laminates without any intermediate steps, and the new application will link chemically with the previous one to form a powerful chemical bond. For a tack-free surface on the final application, coat the resin with polyvinyl alcohol (PVA) or seal it with plastic wrap.

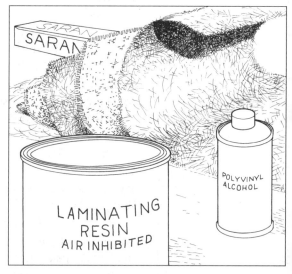

2 Finishing resin is identical to laminating resin, but with an additive that "floats" to the surface of the curing resin. This surfactant (once wax, but now usually a drying oil) seals the resin from the air, thus allowing the surface to fully cure to a tack-free, sandable state.

Use finishing resin for laminate jobs that can be done in a single operation. Finishing resin can also be used for the final layer of a multilayer lamination.

ORTHO, ISO, OR VINYLESTER?

FOR THE FIRST 30 YEARS OF FIBERGLASS BOAT MANUFACTURING, the only resin widely in use was *orthophthalic* resin. Ortho resin was cheap, easy to work with, and had no apparent failings—until fiberglass boats began to blister.

Isophthalic resin, slightly more expensive, has largely replaced ortho resin in boat manufacturing because it seems less prone to blistering, probably due to its higher solvent resistance. A packaged polyester resin sold for repair work, if it is good quality, will likely be iso resin.

Vinylester has long been used in performance boats because of its superior adhesion qualities and impact resistance, but its superiority as a moisture barrier has led to more widespread use. Many new boat manufacturers now use vinylester laminating resin and vinylester gelcoat in their quest to produce blister-resistant hulls. For repair work calling for polyester resin, vinylester's better adhesion makes it a good choice.

HOW MUCH CATALYST?

The catalyst for polyester resin is methyl ethyl ketone peroxide, or MEKP. Do not confuse MEKP with the common solvent MEK; they are *not* the same.

Polyester resin usually requires 1 to 2 percent of hardener by volume (follow the manufacturer's instructions). As a rule of thumb, four drops of hardener will catalyze 1 ounce of resin at 1 percent. Be certain to stir the catalyst in thoroughly or part of the resin will be undercured, weakening the lay-up.

You can adjust the cure time by adding more or less catalyst. Temperature, weather, and the thickness of the laminate all affect curing times. Some experimentation is generally required. The mix shouldn't kick (start to harden) in less than 30 minutes. Hardening in about two hours is probably ideal, but overnight is just as good unless the wait will hold you up. *Always err on the side of too little catalyst;* if you add too much, the resin will "cook," resulting in a weak lamination.

FIBERGLASS MATERIAL

Fiberglass material is exactly what it sounds like, a weave of glass fibers. For boat construction and repair, the glass comes in chopped-strand mat, roving, and cloth.

Chopped-strand mat.
Chopped-strand mat is made up of irregular lengths of glass strands glued together randomly. Generally speaking, *CSM* is the easiest fabric to shape, gives the best resin-to-glass ratio, yields the smoothest surface, is the most watertight, and is the least subject to delamination, but the short fibers do not provide the tensile strength of a woven material.

Mat is sold by the yard from a roll and comes in various weights designated in ounces per square *foot;* 1½-ounce mat is a good choice for general use.

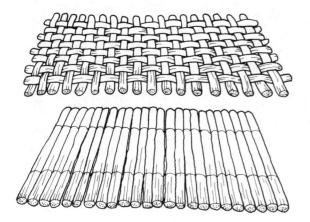

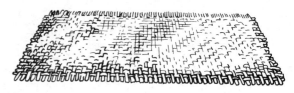

Roving.

Roving is parallel, flat bundles of continuous glass strands. In *unwoven roving* parallel bundles are cross-stitched together; *woven roving* assembles the bundles in two directions in a loose weave.

The straight, continuous strands in unwoven roving add excellent strength in the direction of the strands but little strength perpendicular to them. For hull and deck repairs, woven roving is usually a better choice because it provides full strength in two directions and good strength in all directions. (You can accomplish the same thing by rotating the orientation of alternating laminates of unwoven roving, but unless you need additional strength in a particular direction, using woven roving is simpler.)

Roving laminated to roving, either unwoven or woven, is unacceptably easy to peel apart. *Always* bind layers of roving together by using a layer of mat between each layer of roving.

For most repairs, select 18-ounce roving. That may sound heavy relative to 1½-ounce mat, but don't be confused. Weight designations for mat are per square foot, while for roving (and cloth) they are per square *yard*; 18-ounce roving weighs the same as 2-ounce mat.

Fiberglass cloth.

Fiberglass cloth looks like shiny canvas but not woven as tightly. Cloth is stronger for its weight than roving, less prone to pulling and unraveling in the laminating process, and the finished product looks better. While manufacturers generally use alternating layers of mat and roving, mat and cloth is a better choice for most repair work.

Cloth is commonly available in weights from 4 to 20 ounces. For any boat over 15 feet, there will be little, if any, fiberglass work that you cannot do with 1½-ounce mat and 10-ounce cloth. If you have a choice, buy 38-inch width.

OTHER MATERIALS

GLASS ISN'T THE ONLY MATERIAL THAT CAN be combined with resin. Increasingly, boatbuilders are using "exotic" materials to create composites with special characteristics—light weight, rigidity (or flexibility), impact resistance, tensile strength, or others. These materials include graphite (carbon fiber), Kevlar, polypropylene, xynole-polyester, Dynel, and ceramic. None of these is essential for the typical hull or deck repair. You should understand a material's strengths and weaknesses before you use it.

GRINDING IS ESSENTIAL

During the lay-up process, each application of resin links chemically with the previous application to form a solid structure—as though all the layers were saturated at once. The layer-cake look of fiberglass is deceiving; a better analogy is Jell-O salad—the fruit may be in layers, but the encapsulating Jell-O is solid. Chemical linking between resin layers occurs because each layer is applied before the previous one fully cures (the reason for using air-inhibited resin).

Unfortunately, no matter how strong the laminate-to-laminate bond, the initial bond of any *repair* is mechanical, not chemical. This need not weaken the repair as long as the surface is properly prepared. That means grinding.

1 Before grinding, always wash the area thoroughly with a dewaxing solvent. The original fiberglass will have traces of mold release on the outer surface and wax surfactant on the inner surface. If you fail to remove the wax first, grinding will drag it into the bottom of the surface scratches and weaken the bond.

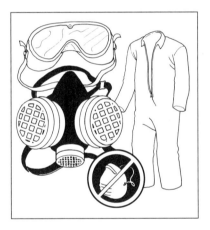

2 Protect your eyes with goggles and your lungs with a good dust mask. A paper mask is inadequate for all but the smallest grinding task. Long sleeves will reduce skin irritation.

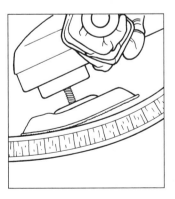

3 Outline the area of the bond and grind inside the outline with a disk sander loaded with a 36-grit disk. Tilt the sander so that only one side of the disk is touching the surface and the dust is thrown away from you.

4 Brush away the dust and wipe the area with an acetone-dampened rag. The surface should have a uniform dull look; if any areas remain glossy, make another pass over them with the sander.

THE BASICS OF FIBERGLASS LAY-UP

PREPARATION

1 Dewax and grind the surface the lay-up will be applied to. Specific types of repairs—detailed later—require additional surface prep.

2 Protect all surrounding surfaces by masking. Waxing below the repair area will make unanticipated runs easier to remove.

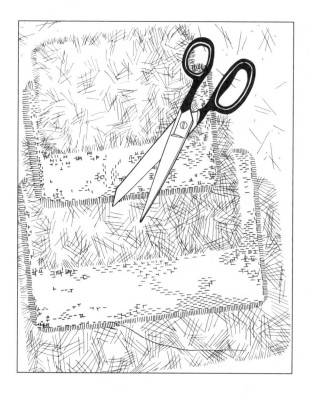

3 Cut the fiberglass pieces to the correct size and lay them out in the order you will be applying them. As a rule, apply the smallest piece first, the largest piece last. Always start and finish with mat.

APPLYING THE INITIAL LAYER

1 Catalyze the resin and mix it thoroughly.

2 Hold the first layer of fiberglass in place and pencil a line around it. Use a throw-away brush to coat the outlined area with resin.

3 Apply the first layer of mat to the wetted surface. On a vertical surface, use masking tape to help hold the fabric in place. Use a squeegee to smooth the mat and press it into the resin.

4 With a brush or a roller, wet the mat with resin until it is uniformly transparent. White areas are dry spots and require additional resin. Brush or roll gently to avoid moving the fabric or introducing bubbles.

ADDITIONAL LAYERS

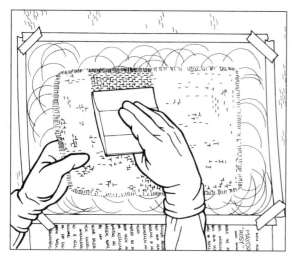

1 Apply the next layer—cloth or roving—on top of the saturated mat. Smooth it against the mat with a squeegee.

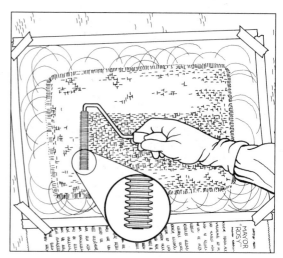

2 Wet out the cloth with resin. Use a squeegee or a grooved roller to compact the laminates and force any air bubbles to the surface. Remove excess resin with the squeegee.

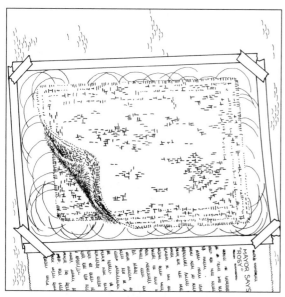

3 If the weather is cool or the repair area is small, you can apply up to two more layers without risk of the cure generating so much heat that it cooks the resin or warps the repair.

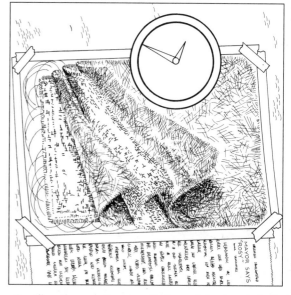

4 Allow the resin time to gel, then mix fresh resin and apply two (or more) additional layers, repeating this process until all the layers have been laminated.

FINISHING

1 For a smoother finish, roll an additional coat of resin over the final layer of material.

2 After the last coat of resin kicks, brush or spray on an unbroken coating of polyvinyl alcohol (PVA) to seal the surface so it will cure fully. This isn't necessary if you use finishing resin for the last coat.

WORKING OVERHEAD

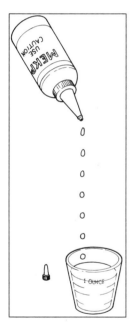

1 Alternative application techniques are required to laminate fiberglass overhead. Mix a small batch of resin, adding more catalyst than usual, and use it to wet the repair area.

2 For an overhead repair, always work with small pieces of fabric. Roll the first piece of mat onto a dowel or a cardboard tube, and wait for the resin to start to kick. When the surface feels tacky, carefully position the edge of the mat and unroll it, taking care to keep it smooth. The tacky resin will hold the mat in place while you saturate it with fresh resin. Use a roller or squeegee to distribute the resin.

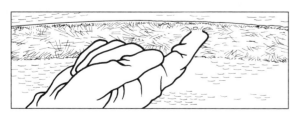

3 When the surface of the mat is tacky, you can unroll the next layer of fabric onto it, again taking care to keep it smooth. Saturate this layer with fresh resin. Repeat this step for each layer until all the laminates are in place.

WHEN TO USE EPOXY

Epoxy is almost always better than polyester resin for repair work because the mechanical bond it forms—the weakest link in any repair job—is stronger. Laminate made with epoxy is also superior— stronger and more durable—but because the cost of epoxy is more than twice that of polyester, manufacturers rarely use it for laminating. For repair work the additional expense is less significant, and the added strength is well worth the cost.

Do not use epoxy if the repair will be finished with gelcoat. While epoxy bonds tenaciously to polyester, the reverse is not true; the bond between polyester gelcoat and an underlying epoxy repair will not be strong. If the surface will be gelcoated, use polyester resin for the repair.

SELECTING EPOXY

Don't buy epoxy by the tube.

Select an epoxy formulated for boatbuilding. The two most common brands are West System (Gougeon Brothers) and System Three, but there are others. The main difference you are likely to notice between competing brands is the mix ratio, but metered pumps tend to make this difference of little consequence.

ADDITIVES

For saturating fiberglass laminates, use the epoxy as it comes—catalyzed, of course—but for bonding and filling, additives thicken the epoxy and give it specific characteristics. Three of these are especially useful for hull and deck repairs.

Fibers. Fibers added to epoxy will thicken it for filling and for bonding where there is a gap between the surfaces being bonded. You can snip glass cloth diagonally to generate short fibers for small putty needs, but for more than that buy packaged microfiber filler. Fiber fillers are easy to mix, provide good strength, and have excellent finish properties.

Microballoons. Microballoons are tiny hollow beads of plastic. Added to epoxy to produce a fairing compound, microballoons yield a putty that spreads and sands easily. Microballoons reduce the strength of the epoxy and should not be used for bonding or laminating. Also avoid using microballoons below the waterline because the resulting putty is porous and will absorb water.

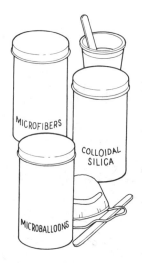

Colloidal Silica. Silica is perhaps the most versatile of fillers. It provides better strength than microfibers and it doesn't affect the permeability of the cured epoxy. Silica-thickened putty cures with a rough texture and resists abrasion—including sanding.

MIXING

Metering pumps.

While polyester requires only a few drops of catalyst per ounce of resin to start the chemical reaction, the combination ratio for epoxy is much less one-sided. The resin-to-hardener ratio is typically at least five to one, but some formulations call for a two-to-one mix. Epoxy manufacturers typically have calibrated pumps available that will meter out the correct ratio—one pump of hardener to one pump of resin. Epoxy is very sensitive to mix ratio, so the purchase of metering pumps is strongly recommended. Stir the two parts together *thoroughly*, using a flat mixing stick to scrape the sides, bottom, and corners of the container.

Regulating cure time.

Unlike polyester, the cure time of epoxy cannot be adjusted by altering the amount of hardener. The specified proportion of hardener must always be used. However, epoxy manufacturers generally offer at least two hardeners—fast and slow—and they often have additional hardener formulations for special requirements, such as tropical use. Pot life varies with ambient temperature, but you will quickly learn how much time is available. Limit batch size to the amount of epoxy you can use in that amount of time. Epoxy cures faster in the pot, so the quicker you apply it, the longer you will have to work it.

Thickening.

Always add the thickening agent after the resin and hardener have been mixed. Stir in the thickener until the mixture reaches the desired consistency.

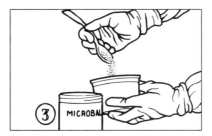

PRECAUTIONS

People in significant numbers develop a sensitivity to epoxy so that any exposure results in skin irritation and rash. Avoiding all skin contact is the safest course. Wear plastic gloves when working with epoxy. Goggles are recommended.

Avoid breathing the fumes of curing epoxy. Be sure you have good ventilation.

The heat generated by curing epoxy is sufficient to melt a plastic container and may even ignite into flames if you leave the mixture in the pot too long. If the mixture begins to heat up, put it outside—away from anything flammable—until it cools.

LAMINATING WITH EPOXY

1 Do *not* use chopped-strand mat when laminating with epoxy resin. The binder holding the strands together may react with the epoxy, affecting both the adhesion and the permeability of the epoxy. Epoxy is a strong enough adhesive to bind cloth to cloth without risk of delamination, and multiple layers of fiberglass cloth create an extremely strong laminate.

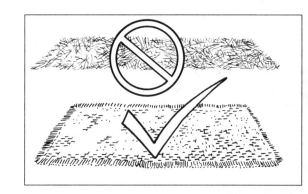

2 Prepare and wet the repair area as with polyester resin, but then thicken some epoxy to a catsup consistency with colloidal silica. Paint the repair area with the thickened epoxy. This serves much the same function as an initial layer of mat, filling voids and depressions and providing a good contact area for the initial layer of cloth.

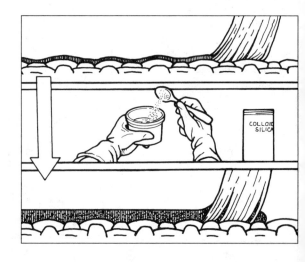

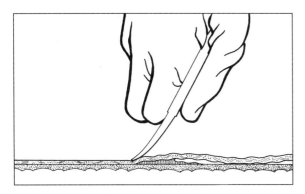

3 Put the initial layer of cloth in position and use the squeegee to smooth it. Wet it out thoroughly.

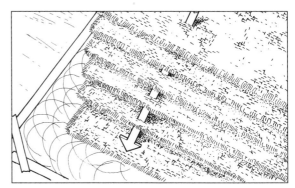

4 Place, wet, and smooth succeeding layers until you achieve the desired thickness. As long as the previous application has not reached a solid cure, which generally takes several hours, you can continue to add layers without any intermediate steps—cleaning, sanding, etc. Each application will chemically bond to the previous one. (If you let the epoxy reach solid cure, you must scrub then grind the surface before applying the next layer—so plan your repair accordingly.)

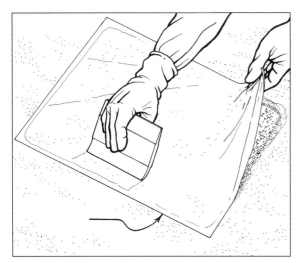

5 For smoothest results, cover the last layer with *peel ply*—a coated fabric epoxy will not adhere to—and use a squeegee to smooth and press the fabric. Scrape away excess epoxy.

6 When the epoxy has cured thoroughly, remove the peel ply; the waxy amine blush that normally appears on the surface of cured epoxy will peel away on the fabric. If you haven't used peel ply, scrub the cured epoxy with a Scotchbrite pad and water before applying any coating (paint, etc.).

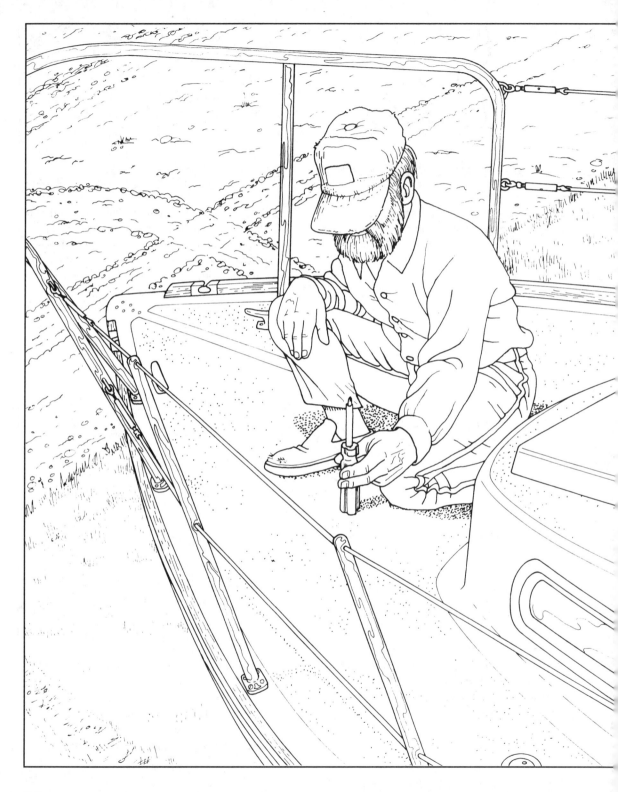

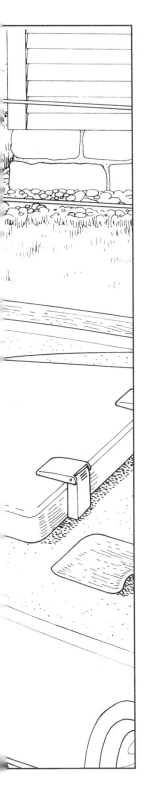

CORE PROBLEMS

Cored deck (or hull) is a sandwich construction of wood, plastic foam, or other material captured between two fiberglass skins. As long as the skins are attached to the core, this box-beam-like construction provides the desirable combination of stiffness and light weight; but if the bond between the skins and the core fails, the three components, none stiff individually, simply slide over each other as they flex—like leaf springs on an old car—and the stiffness is lost. Unfortunately the skin-to-core bond fails often.

This problem is made worse by moisture. Relaxed vigilance in maintaining the seal around deck-mounted hardware leads to water finding its way to the core. The core material, porous by design, absorbs the water like a sponge. The tenuous grip the resin had on dry core material is soon lost, not unlike a bandage releasing its grip under water.

It gets worse still. When water finds its way into the cavity between the two skins, it is captured as surely as if you had poured it into a capped jug. Once core gets wet, it is likely to stay wet until you take steps to dry it out.

The simplest of core problems is delamination, often signaled by cracking sounds underfoot when you walk on the deck. Sound also provides a clue to the more serious problem of wet core, but in this case the sound is a squish. Water may also squirt or weep from around hardware or a crack in the skin when you step on the wet area. Wet core should be attended to immediately. If left unattended until the deck feels spongy underfoot, the core is probably rotten and the repair job you face formidable.

The message here is simple: keep the deck well sealed and you won't need most of the information in this chapter. If it is already too late for this advice, then here are the instructions for dealing with core problems.

DELAMINATION

S ailboats rarely suffer from delamination except where core is involved. Between laminates of fiberglass, the bond is chemical (as long as the fabricator didn't delay too long between layers) and strong, but between the skins and the core the bond is mechanical and weak. Most often the outer skin separates from the core.

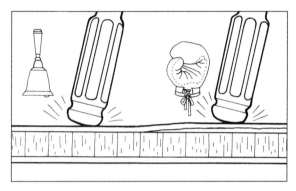

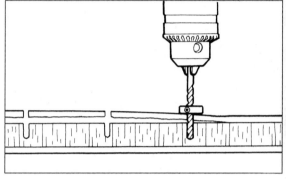

1 Map the area of delamination. Use a plastic mallet or the handle of a screwdriver to tap the area, listening for the telltale difference in sound. A void will have a dull, flat tone compared to the resonance of solid laminate.

2 Drill several small holes ($^3/_{16}$") just inside the outline. The holes should penetrate the outer skin and the core, but not the inner skin. Check the core material pulled out by the drill to make sure the core is dry. Poke at the core through the holes with a piece of wire to make sure it is solid. If the core is wet or spongy, additional steps are required—see the next two sections.

3 Identify the lowest hole in the pattern and mark it. With sheet metal screws, close all the other holes except one. Place the square-cut end of a piece of vinyl hose tightly over the marked hole and blow on the hose. Air should pass freely out the one open hole. Move one screw, closing the tested hole and opening another one, and check again for air flow. Check every hole. If any holes fail to pass air, drill a new hole 1 inch farther inside the outline and test it.

If any hole is more than 5 or 6 inches from another one, drill an intermediate hole to limit the between-hole distance to about 6 inches.

Remove the screws.

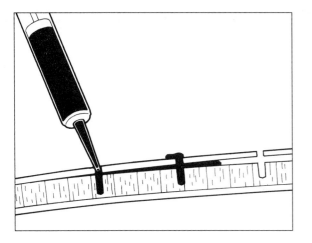

4 Mix an appropriate batch of epoxy and thicken it slightly—to catsup consistency—with colloidal silica. Cut the tip of an epoxy syringe (available from your epoxy supplier) at an angle and fill the syringe with the mix. Insert the tip tightly into the marked hole and inject the void with epoxy. As each hole begins to discharge epoxy, close it with tape. If you flow the epoxy in from the highest hole rather than injecting it from the lowest, you run the risk of trapping air resulting in an incomplete bond.

On a large void, you will need to inject a section at a time, using one of the outlet holes from the previous injection as the new fill hole. Keep flowing epoxy into the void until it flows out all the holes.

5 Weight (horizontal surface) or brace (vertical surface) the outer skin to compress it against the core. Take care not to deflect the skin out of shape. Use wax paper under the weights or braces, and pick up any excess epoxy that vents from the holes.

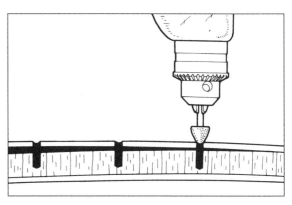

6 Repair the holes like any other surface damage. In this case, the underlying epoxy does not preclude the use of gelcoat to patch the holes as long as the epoxy is scrubbed clean of amine and the surface is dimpled and roughened with a drill-mounted grinding point.

SOLID LAMINATE DELAMINATION

DELAMINATION FOUND IN SOLID LAMINATE should be analyzed carefully. The cause is almost always excessive flex, which tears the bond between the laminates. Occasionally the lay-up schedule is too light—i.e., too few layers of glass—for the duty required of the laminate. In such a case, repair efforts must also include adding additional layers or perhaps other stiffening actions to prevent any recurrence.

More often the delamination is the result of an "incident," usually a collision with a solid object. Provided there is no indication of any substantive damage to the glass fabric, the repair detailed for delamination of the top skin from the core—the most common circumstance—can be used with equal success to treat delamination in solid lay-up.

If the drill bit brings out wet core material, it must be dried out before it can be rebonded to the skin.

SMALL AREA

Often the wet area is limited to the immediate proximity of the source of the moisture. Depending upon the core material and the extent of the saturation, one or all of the following drying methods may be applied.

Vacuum.
A shop vac will remove water from the cavity and extract some moisture from the core. Vacuum bagging using an air compressor and a vacuum generator will be more effective at drying the core. A refrigeration vacuum pump might also be adapted by threading a nipple into the skin.

Flushing.
Flooding the cavity with acetone can be effective. The acetone combines with water, carrying it away. Acetone left behind quickly evaporates, leaving dry core. Always keep in mind that acetone is extremely flammable.

Heat.
A hair dryer or a heat gun played over the wet area will effect some drying. (Be careful not to overheat the laminate; if it's too hot to touch, it's too hot.) The core must be sufficiently exposed for the heat-evaporated moisture to escape; otherwise the moisture simply rises to the underside of the skin and is reabsorbed by the core when the heat is removed. To expose the core, perforate the skin and the core with a pattern of holes drilled about every inch. Don't use a heat gun if you have flushed the core with acetone.

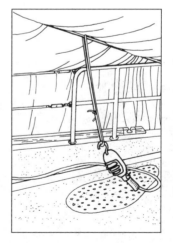

Dry air.
Simply leaving the core exposed will result in drying if the air is dry. Drill the pattern of holes in the wet core and leave the boat in a heated garage or other enclosed storage area for a few weeks, or tent the damaged area and leave a light bulb burning inside the tent to reduce the humidity.

LARGE AREA

If a large section of core is saturated, the only practical solution is to remove one of the skins to fully expose the core so it can be dried thoroughly.

Removing the inner skin.
Removing the inner skin is the preferable way of gaining access to saturated core because it leaves the glossy and the nonskid surfaces of the exterior hull or deck unmarked. Gaining access to the inner skin may require removal of furniture or an inner liner. If access will be very difficult, you are likely to be better off removing the outer skin instead.

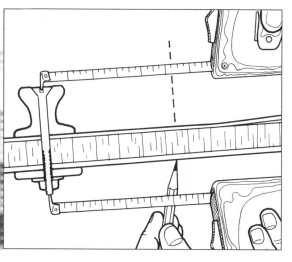

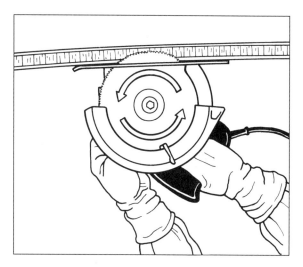

1 Outline the damaged area with straight lines and transfer this outline to the inner skin. This is easily done by making a paper pattern and measuring corner distances to some through-deck feature—a cleat-mounting bolt, for example.

2 Drill an exploratory hole to determine how far the underside of the outer skin is from the surface of the inner skin. Fit a circular saw with a carbide-tipped plywood bit and set the cutting depth to slightly less to allow for some variation in this dimension. Cut around the outline.

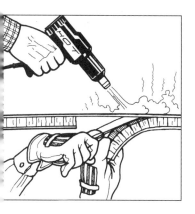

3 Finish the cut through the core with a razor knife. If the top-skin bond is completely broken, the cutout will drop out. If not, find a loose corner and pry down, then use a sharpened flexible putty knife as a chisel to free the rest of the core. Heat applied to the outer skin may help.

Removing the outer skin.

If access to the inner skin is difficult, removing the outer skin may be the better way to expose a saturated core.

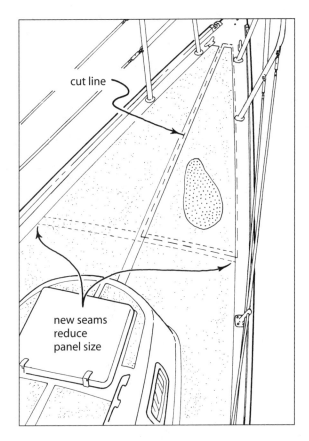

cut line

new seams
reduce
panel size

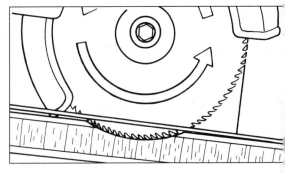

2 Set the cut depth to the *thickness of the skin only* and cut around the outline.

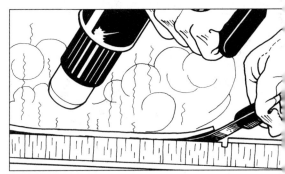

1 Plan your cut wisely. When you replace the skin, the cut will be much easier to hide if it is in a smooth section of the deck rather than across the nonskid. On the other hand, if you are going to cover the repair with a nonskid overlay, you will want to confine the cuts to the nonskid area. If the wet core is only on one side of the foredeck, adding a smooth seam to the nonskid on the centerline (when you reinstall the skin) will allow you to cut away a smaller section of deck.

3 If the skin is still partially bonded, pry up a free corner and use a sharpened flexible putty knife as a chisel to free it completely. Heat applied to the skin may help. Unless the skin is badly damaged, save it; you will reinstall it when the core is dry.

DAMAGED CORE

Once you have exposed the core, you may discover that it has already begun to deteriorate. In that case, replacement is the only sensible course.

1 Chisel the damaged core from the inner skin. Or . . .

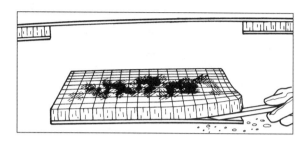

2 . . . Use a utility knife (for balsa or foam) or a saw (for plywood) to cut around the damaged area, taking care not to cut the inner skin. Remove the core with a chisel, shaving the inner skin completely clean.

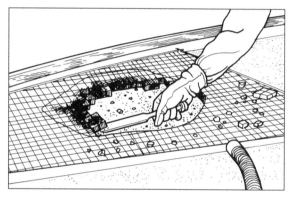

3 Make a paper pattern of the removed section and use it to cut a new piece of core. It is important to use core material the same as the original, both in type and thickness, if possible. Balsa and foam are available from specialty suppliers. If the core is plywood, use only marine-grade plywood for the repair. Sand the surface of the plywood and clean it with a solvent-dampened rag.

    Dry-fit the core into the cavity, trimming as necessary. When you are satisfied with the fit, grind the inner surface of the skin.

4 Wet out the surface of the skin, the appropriate surface of the new core, and all core edges (old and new).

5 Thicken the epoxy to mayonnaise consistency with colloidal silica, and coat all the bonding surfaces generously. Install the new core.

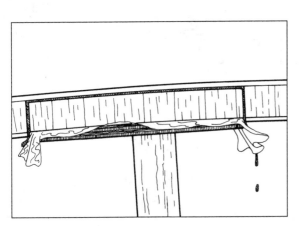

6 Brace the core in position. Or . . .

7 . . . Weight the core in position. Protect the weights (or braces) with plastic sheeting or wax paper. A sand-filled garbage bag makes an excellent weight for this purpose because it conforms to the shape of the deck. The core should be solidly bedded in the thickened epoxy, and epoxy should squeeze out the cut line all the way around the new section. Remove the squeeze-out, then let the epoxy cure fully before removing the weights.

If the old skin was in poor condition, you will have to lay up a new one with glass cloth and epoxy, but most of the time the old skin can be simply put back in place. Whether you have dried the old core or replaced it, reinstallation of the removed skin is the same.

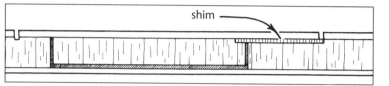

shim

1 Dry fit the removed section. Grind or shim until the skin section realigns properly with the surrounding surfaces.

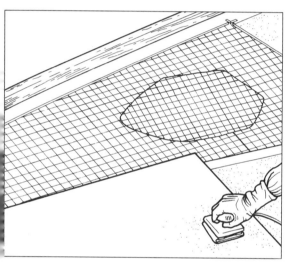

2 Sand the surface of the core and the underside of the skin. Clean with a solvent-dampened rag.

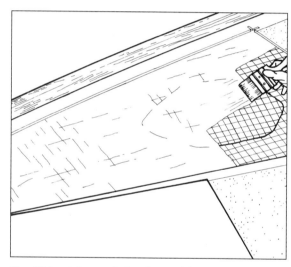

3 Wet out the sanded surfaces with epoxy.

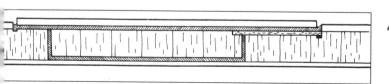

4 Thicken the epoxy to mayonnaise consistency with colloidal silica and coat both surfaces. Be sure to apply enough epoxy putty to solidly fill the space between the skin and the core.

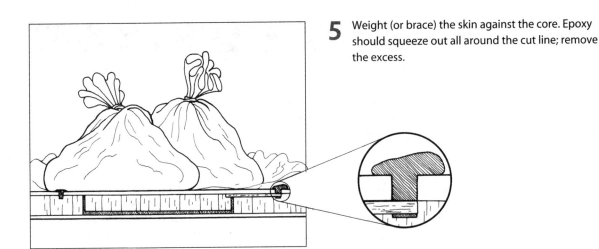

5 Weight (or brace) the skin against the core. Epoxy should squeeze out all around the cut line; remove the excess.

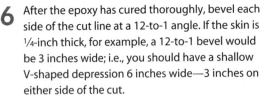

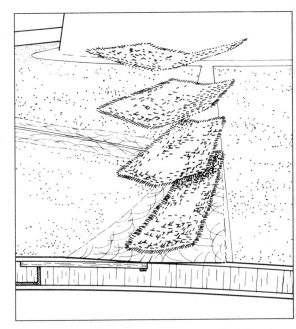

6 After the epoxy has cured thoroughly, bevel each side of the cut line at a 12-to-1 angle. If the skin is ¼-inch thick, for example, a 12-to-1 bevel would be 3 inches wide; i.e., you should have a shallow V-shaped depression 6 inches wide—3 inches on either side of the cut.

7 Cut fiberglass cloth into narrow strips (tape) and laminate them into the depression with epoxy resin. Each strip should be about 1 inch wider than the previous one. Remember not to use mat with epoxy. Sand the cured surface and paint it or cover it with nonskid overlay.

STRENGTHENING

Fiberglass boats sometimes flex alarmingly under pressure or exhibit a pattern of surface cracks around hardware, in corners, or at other stress points. These can both be signs of excessive weakness.

Fiberglass laminate is easily strengthened by adding additional layers. Strengthening layers are most often added to the inner surface of the hull or deck.

1 Outline the area to be strengthened. Dewax and grind the surface thoroughly to prepare it.

2 Cut multiple layers of fiberglass cloth, the first to the size of the outline, then each a little smaller than the previous. If you are reinforcing a large area, keep the cloth pieces small enough to handle—generally not much larger than 1 square yard if you're working alone. Overlap joints on an inside surface; butt them if you are adding laminates to the outside surface.

3 Follow the laminating procedures detailed in "Laminate Repair." Use epoxy resin. Epoxy is stronger than polyester resin, and strength is what you're after. Epoxy also binds the new laminates to the old more securely.

Glass-reinforced plastic is by nature flexible, and excessive flexing more often indicates inadequate stiffness rather than inadequate strength. Adding layers does stiffen the area as well, but when strengthening is not required, stiffening is usually better accomplished with a sandwich construction.

Doubling the thickness makes a panel eight times as stiff. This is the reason the manufacturer put core in the deck. You can add a layer of core and a thin inner skin to a panel to stiffen it, but often a reinforcing member or two will do the same job with less work and less weight.

Called "hat-shaped stiffeners," reinforcing members are rib- or stringer-like fiberglass constructions formed over a strip of wood or other material. Judiciously spaced, hat-shaped stiffeners are quite effective.

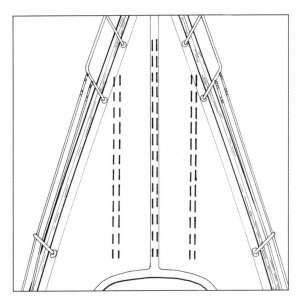

1 Decide where the stiffeners will go. Generally they should run parallel to the long dimension of the area you are stiffening. The number of stiffeners required will depend on the flexibility of the panel; add them one at a time until you are satisfied with the result.

2 Select a core material. Wood adds some strength, but most of the stiffness comes from the box construction, so an easier-to-form core material such as foam, hose, or cardboard may be a better choice. If you use wood, taper the ends to avoid creating a hard spot where the stiffener ends.

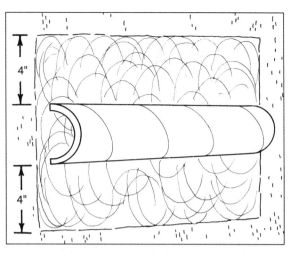

3 Dewax the panel where the first stiffener will be attached. Grind an area about 8 inches wider than the width of the core material.

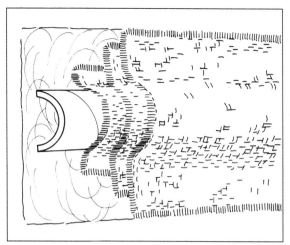

4 Cut a strip of 10-ounce cloth wide enough to extend out 2 inches on either side of the core. Cut a second strip 2 inches wider and a third 2 inches wider still. The recommended height-to-skin-thickness ratio is 30 to 1, so three layers of 10-ounce cloth (which yield a cured thickness of about 0.120 inch) are generally sufficient for stiffeners up to about 3½ inches high. If you want extra layers for added assurance, cut each strip 2 inches wider than the previous one. Be sure to grind a wider area.

5 Tack the core material in place with hot glue or quick-set epoxy. Since the glass cloth won't form into a sharp corner, it is good practice to put an epoxy-putty fillet along the edges of the core.

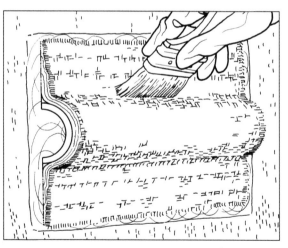

6 Apply the laminates over the core, wetting them out with epoxy resin. (Polyester resin is inferior for this use for reasons already mentioned, but if you use polyester, substitute mat for the odd-numbered layers.)

HULL REPAIRS

Fiberglass hulls are incredibly durable. They don't rot like wood or corrode like steel. They don't dry out and open seams. They don't get worms. In fact, after 35 years of production-line manufacture, the only insidious problem to surface in these boats is blistering, and even that affects only a small percentage of hulls.

If you keep the hull away from solid objects such as rocks, docks, and other boats, required repairs are likely to be limited to restoring the surface gloss. Unfortunately avoiding the occasional "kiss" sounds simpler than it really is. Boats aren't always where you think they are. Underwater obstructions aren't always charted. And rare is the skipper who hasn't watched in disbelief as his boat—a moment before in complete control—suddenly rushes sideways for the dock. Even impeccable navigation and iron-fisted control doesn't prevent another captain's lapse from leaving you with broken glass.

Because the hull is relatively featureless compared with the deck, hull repairs are generally less complicated. But they are more visible; a poor topsides repair can stand out like a shirt-pocket ink stain. You must take the time to fair the patch and match the color for the repair to be invisible.

While it is true that the hull is the part of the boat that "keeps the ocean out," there is no reason to approach hull repair with any greater trepidation than repairing the deck. Prepare the surface properly, which means little more than cleaning and grinding—always grinding—and follow the other steps carefully, and your patch will be just as strong as the surrounding hull, maybe stronger.

GOUGES

In "Restoring the Gloss," we looked at scratch repair, but sometimes an encounter with a sharp, solid object gouges into the underlying laminate. In this instance, the laminate must be repaired before the gelcoat is restored. How you make the repair depends on the extent of the damage.

REPAIRING A SHALLOW GOUGE

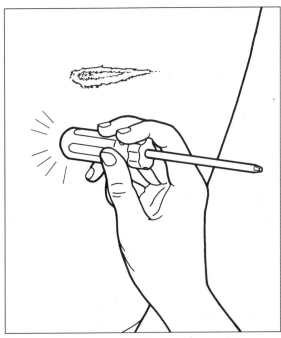

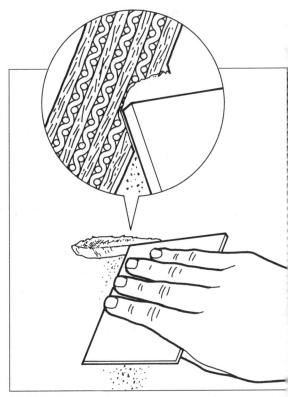

1 Sound the area for delamination. The impact that caused the gouge may have torn the underlying laminates. If the tapping sounds dead rather than resonant, repair the damage as if it were a deep gouge (see below).

2 Use the edge of a cabinet scraper to open the damage, putting a smooth chamfer on each side of the gouge.

3 Catalyze a small quantity of polyester resin and thicken it with chopped glass. Wipe the V with styrene to reactivate the surface of the cured resin, then fill the V to the *bottom* of the gelcoat layer with the thickened resin.

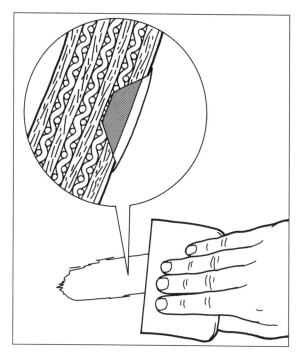

4 When the resin kicks, fill the remaining depression with color-matched gelcoat paste, letting it bulge slightly above the surface. When the gelcoat begins to gel, seal its surface with plastic or a coat of PVA.

5 Allow the gelcoat to cure fully, then fair and polish the repair.

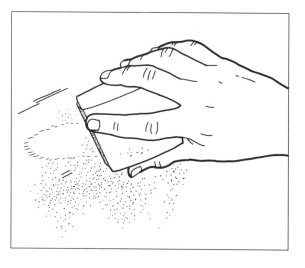

DEEP GOUGES

1 If the damage extends through more than the upper two or three laminates and the gouge is more than a couple of inches long, restoring hull integrity requires replacing the damaged fiberglass. Grind the damaged area into a depression with a 12-to-1 chamfer all around. Grind through all broken layers, using the first undamaged laminate as the bottom of the depression.

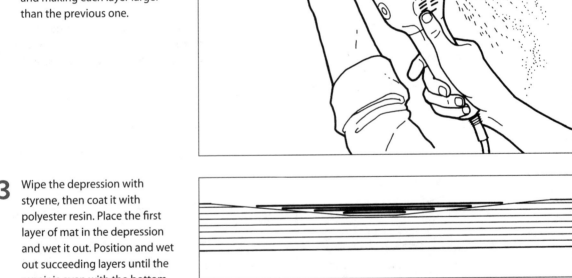

2 Cut alternating layers of mat and cloth, beginning with mat and making each layer larger than the previous one.

3 Wipe the depression with styrene, then coat it with polyester resin. Place the first layer of mat in the depression and wet it out. Position and wet out succeeding layers until the repair is even with the bottom of the gelcoat layer.

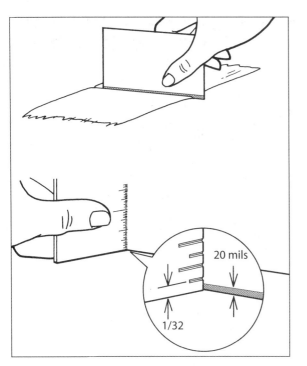

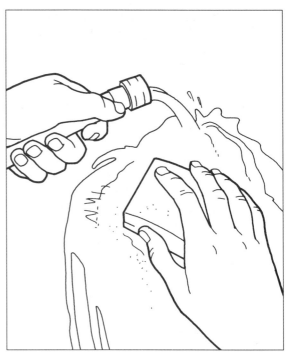

4 When the resin kicks, spray on several coats of color-matched gelcoat (see *Sailboat Refinishing* in this book series), or brush on at least 20 mils of gelcoat paste. Check the thickness by slicing the gelcoat with the edge of a piece of paper and comparing the height of the gelcoat on the paper to a 1/32-inch mark on a ruler, which is about 30 mils.

5 Allow the gelcoat to cure fully, then fair and polish the repair.

WHEN TO USE EPOXY

IF YOU PLAN TO PAINT THE REPAIR RATHER THAN finish it with gelcoat, repair the gouge with epoxy for a better bond. For a shallow gouge, wet the V first with unthickened epoxy, then fill it to the surface with the epoxy thickened with colloidal silica to peanut butter consistency. Try to get the surface as fair as possible before the epoxy kicks because the silica-thickened epoxy is hard to sand, especially without damaging the much softer gelcoat that surrounds it.

For deep gouges, use epoxy and 10-ounce cloth—no mat. Wet out the depression, then coat it with epoxy thickened with colloidal silica to catsup consistency. Apply the layers of cloth and saturate them with epoxy resin. Give the last layer two or three extra coats of resin to completely hide the weave of the cloth. Coating the surface with peel ply is recommended (see "Laminate Repair"). Fairing is likely to be required, but wait until the laminates have fully cured, then thicken some mixed epoxy to peanut butter consistency—use microballoons if the repair is above the waterline, colloidal silica if it is below—and fill all voids and depressions. Sand and paint.

BLISTERS

Fiberglass blisters occur because water passes through the gelcoat. Water-soluble chemicals inside the laminate exert an osmotic pull on water outside, and some water molecules find a way through. As more water is attracted into the enclosed space, internal pressure builds. The water molecules aren't squirted back out the way they came in because they have combined with the attracting chemicals into a solution with a larger molecular structure. Instead, the pressure pushes the covering laminate into a dome—a blister.

There has been a great deal of hysteria about blisters, but the reality is that the number of boats that develop *serious* blister problems is extremely small. An occasional blister or two is *not* a serious problem, any more than is an occasional gouge in the hull. Some boats seem to exhibit a greater propensity to blister, presumably due to the chemical components used and/or the lay-up schedule, but all boats are at some risk. Surveys suggest that about one boat in four develops blisters. Maybe the factory was training a new fiberglass crew the day your boat was built, or the humidity was abnormally high. Or maybe the factory did everything right but somewhere along the way someone sanded the gelcoat excessively, or even sandblasted it to prepare it for bottom paint. It is pointless to speculate. If your boat develops blisters, deal with them; if it doesn't, forget about it.

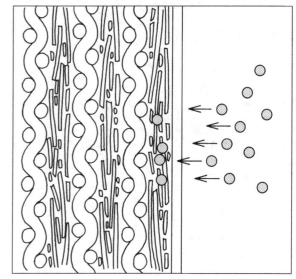

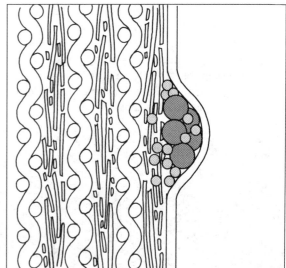

MINOR BLISTERING

1 Open the blister. Wear eye protection; internal pressure can be double that of a champagne bottle, and the fluid that blasts out when you pop the dome is acid. Use a 36-grit disk to grind the blister into a shallow depression.

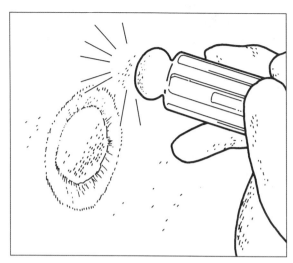

2 Sound around the blister to make sure there isn't any additional delamination.

3 Flush the open blister with water, then scrub it with a TSP solution. Rinse thoroughly.

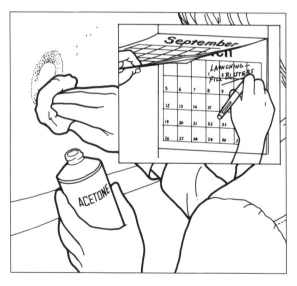

4 Allow the blister to dry for as long as practical. If you dry-store your boat for the winter, open blisters at haulout but don't fill them until launch time. Just before filling, wipe out each blister depression with a rag *dampened* with acetone.

5 Epoxy is the resin to use for blister repairs. It is less permeable than polyester and it forms a much stronger bond. Wet out the cavity with epoxy.

6 For small blisters, thicken epoxy to peanut butter consistency with colloidal silica and fill the cavity, using a squeegee to compress and fair the filler. Silica-thickened epoxy is hard to sand, so fair it well before it kicks: *Never* use microballons or any other hollow or absorbent (talc, for example) fairing compound to fill blisters.

7 Before the repair reaches full cure, paint it with at least two coats of unthickened epoxy.

BOAT POX

Boat pox is a much more serious condition, related to the occasional blister like acne to the occasional pimple. If the bottom of your boat is covered with blisters, filling them won't cure the problem. Pox is a systemic condition and requires remedial action.

1 Examine the bottom as soon as your boat is lifted. Out of the water, blisters can shrink and even disappear altogether. If the bottom is covered with hundreds of blisters, your boat has pox, and the condition will only worsen unless you take the cure.

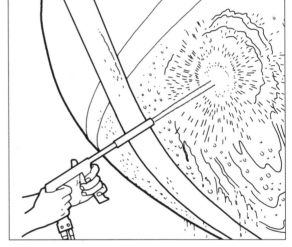

2 Scrub the hull to remove growth, oil, and all other contaminants.

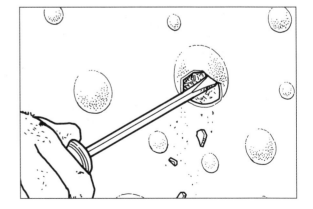

3 Open a few blisters to determine their location. Usually blisters occur between the gelcoat and the first layer of laminate. If they are deeper, see the sidebar.

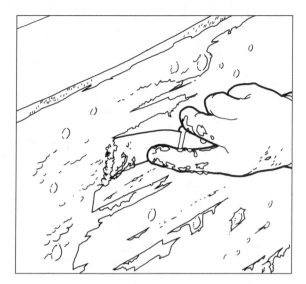

4 Unless you are having the hull machine peeled, chemically strip the bottom of all paint. Curing boat pox requires the removal of *all* the gelcoat below the waterline; but if you do not remove the paint first, gelcoat stripping will contaminate the underlying laminate with paint particles, weakening the bond of the barrier coat.

6 Wash the stripped surface with a stiff brush. It is imperative that all loose bits of gelcoat, paint, and grit are removed. Inspecting the surface with a magnifying glass is not overkill.

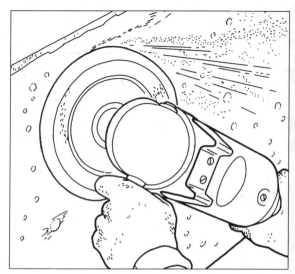

5 Grind away all the gelcoat below the waterline. You cannot just grind open the blisters because a hull with pox is saturated throughout and will not dry out unless the gelcoat is removed. Despite the time required, the best way to strip the gelcoat is with a lightweight disk sander and 24-grit disk on a foam pad. Boatyards prefer to sandblast the hull to remove the gelcoat, but this harsh treatment damages the underlying laminate. If you give in to the expediency of sandblasting, be sure the pressure is low and the sand is directed at the hull at a shallow angle—less than 30 degrees.

Some yards now have peelers that work like a power plane. Set to the appropriate thickness, they shave the gelcoat from the hull in a single pass without any damage to the laminate. If you have the hull peeled, run a 50-grit disk over the peeled surface to remove any ridges and to provide tooth for the barrier coat.

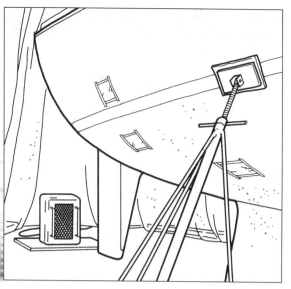

7 With the gelcoat removed and the laminate clean, allow the hull to dry out. This will take at least two weeks in hot temperatures and as long as six months in the cold. Tenting the hull and running fans or a heater will shorten the time.

Keep track of the drying process by taping 6-inch squares of plastic cut from heavy freezer bags to a dozen or more places on the hull—2 or 3 above the waterline. Seal the plastic all around with electrician's tape. Sun on the plastic will cause moisture in the hull to condense on the plastic. Open the plastic and wipe it and the hull dry every few days, then seal it back in place. When condensation ceases to form in any of the test panels on sunny days, the hull is sufficiently dry to reseal.

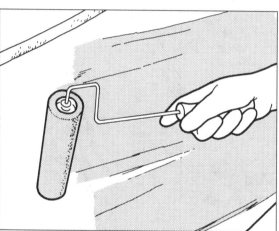

8 Select an epoxy barrier coat product such as InterProtect or West System epoxy and apply it to the recommended thickness—usually 20 mils—according to the manufacturer's instructions.

DEEPER BLISTERS

IT IS FAIRLY COMMON FOR BLISTERS TO OCCUR beneath the first laminate instead of in the laminate/gelcoat junction because of the all-too-common practice of getting the first layer applied to the wet gelcoat, then waiting a day to continue the lay-up. This makes the bond between the first and second laminate weak and susceptible to blistering. Blisters deeper in the laminate are thankfully much rarer, occurring only after less serious blisters have been long ignored.

If you discover that the blisters on your hull are beneath the initial layer of laminate, remove this layer along with the gelcoat. When the hull is dry, apply a replacement layer of 10-ounce cloth to the hull, working with manageable pieces and butt-joining (not overlapping) the sections. Wet each section with epoxy resin, then apply a layer of silica-thickened epoxy before positioning the cloth. Wet out the cloth and seal it with peel-ply and a ply of plastic. Sand and fair the entire surface before applying the barrier coating.

ew things are more disheartening to the boat-owner than staring at the fuzzy edge of broken fiberglass. Most don't realize that the repair of impact damage is usually only a step or two more complicated than filling a gouge or a blister. You don't believe it? If you cut out the damaged area and bevel the edges, then close one side of the hole by laying up a single ply of fiberglass over it,

how is the resulting depression different from a deep gouge except in size? It isn't.

Sometimes, of course, damage is so extensive that a significant section of the hull or deck (or both) has to be rebuilt, but even then the lay-up process is the same. The only difficulty comes in getting the new laminates to take on the right shape.

CUTTING AWAY THE DAMAGED LAMINATE

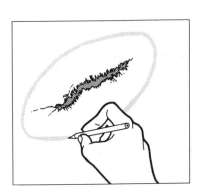

1 Impact damage almost always has some associated delamination. Tap the area to determine the extent of the damage and map it. Enclose the marked area in a circular or oval trace.

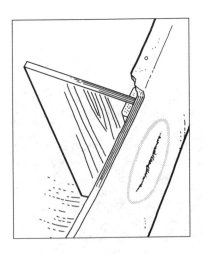

2 Go inside the boat and determine if anything will be in the way when you cut out the damaged section. Sometimes it is best to cut out an offending member; in other cases you may want to leave it intact, cutting the damaged skin free. If you don't have inside access, use a 3- or 4-inch hole saw to remove a circular plug from the hull so you can look and feel inside before making the full cutout.

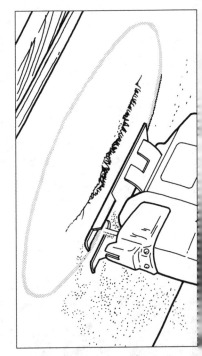

3 Saw around the oval trace. Never try to save damaged fiberglass; always cut it out and replace it with new laminate. You can make the cut with a circular saw fitted with a carbide blade or a cut-off wheel, or with a saber saw fitted with a blade for cutting fiberglass.

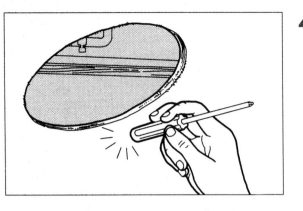

4 Check all the edges to make sure the laminate is solid, and tap again around the hole. Enlarge it if you find any additional delamination.

WORKING FROM THE INSIDE

There are two reasons you should make hull repairs from the inside whenever possible, especially when the damaged area is small. First, you are going to bevel the edge of the hole with a 12-to-1 chamfer. If you repair a 3-inch diameter hole through a ½-inch-thick hull from the outside, you end up with about 15 inches (diameter) of surface damage to refinish, but if you repair it from the inside, you have only a 3-inch hole to refinish.

The second reason is that if you back the hole on the outside with a polished surface, you can in effect create a mold that allows you to lay up the repair the same way the boat was built—gelcoat first—and very little finish work will be required.

1 Dewax the interior surface of the skin around the hole.

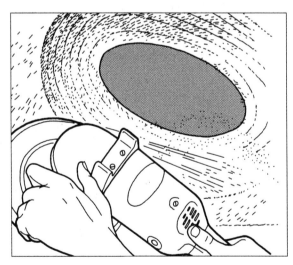

2 Grind the edge of the hole into a 12-to-1 bevel. Also grind a rectangular area of the inner surface a few inches beyond the hole to accommodate a finishing layer of cloth.

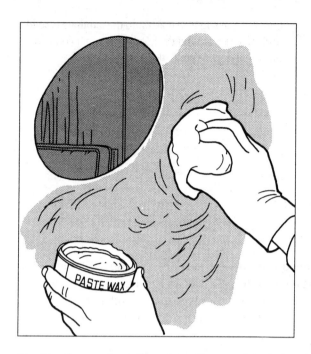

3 Give the exterior surface of the skin around the hole a heavy coat of paste wax, taking care not to get any wax on the edge or inside the hole. The purpose of the wax is to prevent any resin runs from adhering to the exterior surface; paint the wax with PVA to be sure. Mask the area below the hole.

4 Cut a scrap of smooth plastic laminate (Formica) or thin clear acrylic (Plexiglas) a foot larger than the hole. Wax this backer and paint it with PVA, and screw or tape it to the outer surface. If the hull is flat or curving in only one direction in the damage area, the backer will assume the correct curve—check from inside to make sure it seats against the skin all around the hole. If the hull is spherical, i.e., curving in two directions, a sheet backer usually won't work. Where the compound curvature is slight, acrylic screwed to the hull will bend into the correct shape if warmed with a heat gun. Otherwise you will need to make a backer following the instructions in "Taking Off a Mold " below.

5 Cut the fiberglass material to fit the hole. Unless you have reason to follow a different schedule, begin with two layers of 1½- or 2-ounce mat, then alternate mat and 10-ounce cloth. The number of laminates will be determined by the thickness of the hull; you will need roughly one layer for every 1/32 inch. Cut the first layer of mat 1 inch larger than the hole, overlapping the bevel by ½ inch all around. Subsequent pieces should be ½ inch larger all around than the previous one.

6 From inside, spray or brush 20 mils of color-matched gelcoat onto the waxed backer. Check the gelcoat thickness with a toothpick—1/32 inch is about 30 mils.

7 When the gelcoat kicks, wet it with polyester resin and lay up the first two layers of mat and one layer of cloth, compressing them against the gelcoat and working out all voids and bubbles with a resin roller and/or a squeegee.

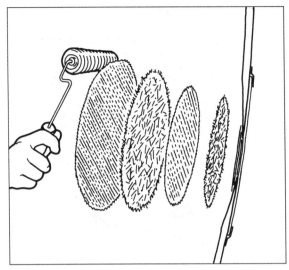

8 Let the first three plies kick, then lay up four additional plies. Never lay up more than four plies at a time or the generated heat may "cook" and weaken the resin. Continue the lay-up four plies at a time until the repair is flush with the interior surface.

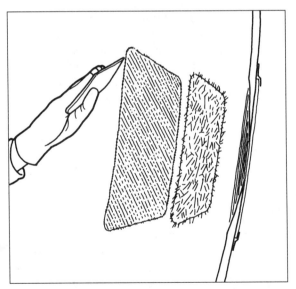

9 For a finished look, cut a rectangular piece of mat and one slightly larger of cloth and apply these over the patch, smoothing them with a squeegee. Seal this top layer with plastic or PVA to allow a full cure.

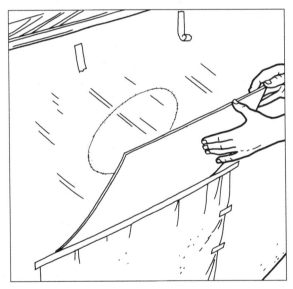

10 Remove the backer from the exterior surface. Fill any imperfections in the new gelcoat with gelcoat paste and allow it to cure fully. Clean the area around the patch, then sand—if necessary—and polish the repair area.

TAKING OFF A MOLD

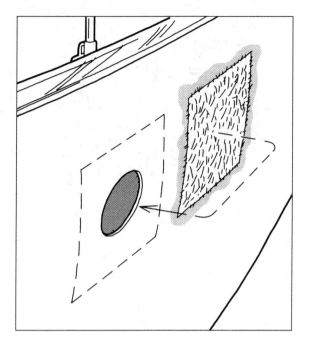

1 At its simplest, taking off a mold involves no more than waxing and release-coating (with PVA) a section of hull with approximately the same contour as the damaged area, usually adjacent to the damage. Coat the waxed area with resin, then lay up two plies of 2-ounce mat. When the lay-up cures, peel it from the hull, coat it with releasing agent, and tape in place over the hole to provide a contoured backer/mold for your repair.

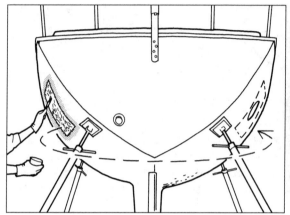

2 For more extensive damage or damage in an area where the shape of the hull is rapidly changing, try taking a mold from the same spot on the other side of the hull. Reversed top to bottom, the molded piece should give you a close approximation of the correct contour. Transfer it while it is still "green," that is before full cure, and it should conform perfectly to the damaged side.

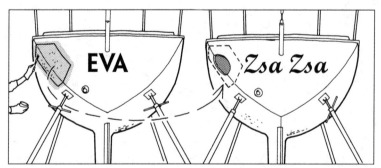

3 When damage is extensive or to an area of the hull with a feature, such as the intersection of the quarter and the transom, taking a mold from the opposite side may not give satisfactory results. If you can locate a sistership with a willing owner, you can lay up a perfect mold. If the mold is sizable, stiffen it with a few hat-shaped stiffeners. Be sure you know how to thoroughly coat a hull to assure release—meaning try it on your own hull first—before you paint someone else's hull with resin.

OUTSIDE REPAIR

If you are going to paint the repair rather than trying to match gelcoat, make the repair from the outside. Working outside is somewhat easier and a lot more comfortable—you're not engulfed in resin fumes or wedged into some impossible corner. If you're not going to finish the repair with gelcoat, you should also use epoxy for its superior bonding strength.

1 Dewax around the hole and grind the edge into a 12-to-1 bevel.

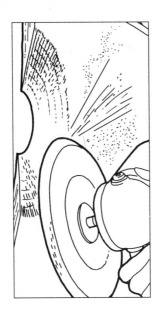

2 Wax the exterior surface of the skin around the hole, taking care not to get any wax on the bevel. Mask the area below the hole.

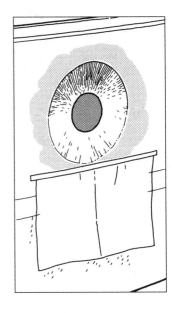

3 Wax and release-coat a scrape of smooth plastic laminate or thin acrylic and *brace* it tightly against the hole from inside. If the hull is flat or curving in only one direction in the damage area, the backer will assume the correct curve. If the hull is spherical, lay up a backer using an adjacent section of the hull as the mold.

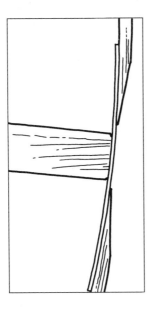

4 If you are using epoxy resin for the repair, cut all your repair pieces from 10-ounce cloth. Mix a batch of epoxy and wet out the first layer of cloth. Use a squeegee to smooth the cloth into position and to remove trapped air. Apply the second layer and wet it out. Squeegee. Repeat this process a layer at a time, mixing fresh epoxy as needed, until the repair is slightly below the surface.

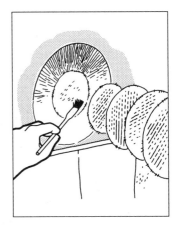

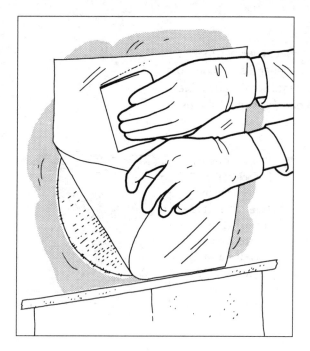

5 Give the final layer a coat or two of epoxy, then cover the surface with peel ply and a layer of plastic and smooth it with the squeegee. Wipe up any squeeze-out.

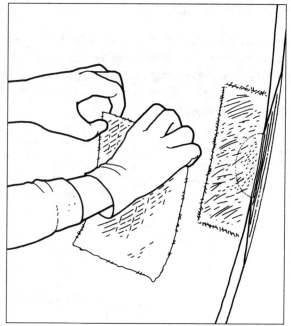

6 Remove the backer from the interior surface and grind the repair and a rectangular area around it. Cut a piece of fiberglass cloth to the size of the ground rectangle and laminate it in place to give the interior of the repair a finished look.

7 Fair the repair with epoxy thickened with micro-balloons (below the waterline, use colloidal silica) and paint.

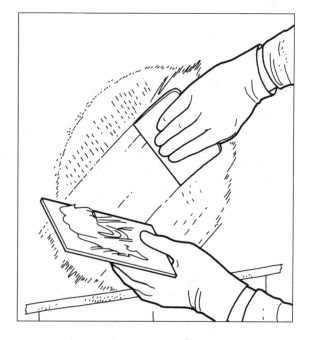

NO INSIDE ACCESS

Often there is a liner or a tank or some other interior obstruction in the damage area that denies you access to the inside of the hull. Except for the need to take extra care when cutting out the damaged section and the effect working from the outside has on the size of the repair requiring finish work, lack of inside access isn't a very big problem.

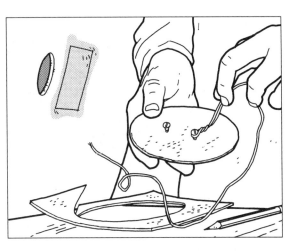

1 Using epoxy resin and two layers of 10-ounce cloth, lay up a backer piece on a waxed and release-coated section of the hull near the damage.

2 When the backer is thoroughly cured, peel it up and trim it to 1 inch larger than the hole. Screw two sheet-metal screws into the backer and twist the ends of a length of wire to the screws to provide a loop handle.

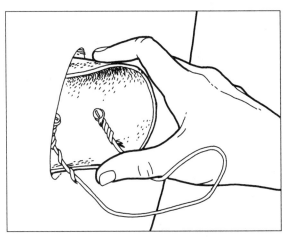

3 Dewax the inside of the skin around the hole by reaching through the hole with a solvent-soaked rag. Sand the dewaxed area with 50-grit paper, again by reaching through the hole. Scrub (with water) and sand the handled surface of the backer.

4 Bend the backer slightly and push it through the hole, holding on to the wire loop. No bending will be necessary if the hole is oval shaped.

5 Thicken a small amount of epoxy to peanut butter consistency with colloidal silica, and butter it onto the perimeter of the backer. Center it and pull it tightly against the opening. Hold it in position with a string tied from the loop to some fixed object. Wipe up all the epoxy that squeezes out and let the bond cure completely.

6 Remove the screws and proceed with the repair as described above.

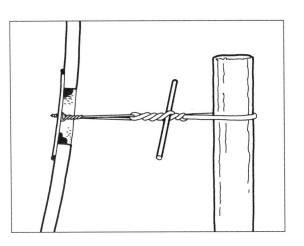

CORED HULL

Impact damage to a cored hull requires repair to the three components—inner skin, core, and outer skin—separately.

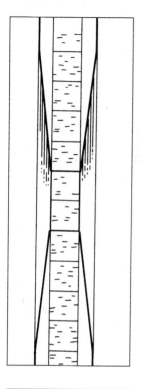

With inside access. Cut out the damage, then grind a 12-to-1 bevel on both skins. Bond a new section of core into the hole, then lay up new skins on either side.

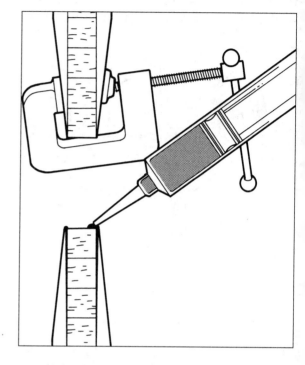

Without inside access. Outline the damage and cut away the outer skin and the core with a router, taking care not to cut the inner skin. With the inner skin now exposed, cut out the damage to it. Bevel both the inner and outer skins, then lay up a new section of inner skin as previously detailed. Install new core on top of the new inner skin and lay up a new outer skin.

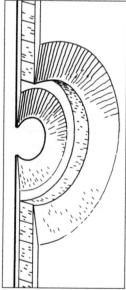

Core delamination. The flexing associated with an impact is likely to result in delamination beyond the area of skin damage. With edge access, inject the separation with epoxy and clamp it until it cures, then complete the repair.

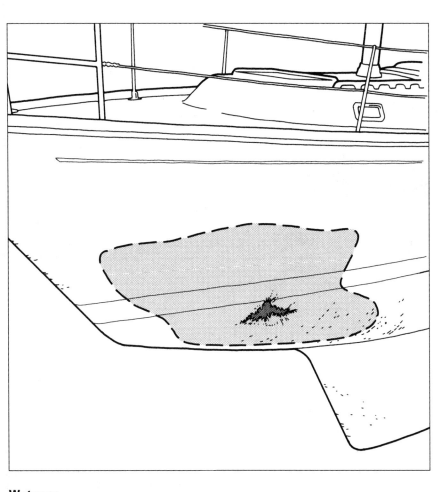

Wet core.

Impact damage below the waterline of a cored hull usually results in wet core. With inside access, determine the extent of the saturation by removing progressively larger sections of the inner skin. Let the core dry or replace it, then complete the repair normally.

Without interior access, it is the outer skin you will have to remove. If the damage to the outer skin is small but the area of saturation large—you should be able to tell by tapping the hull—you may do better to remove the large section of skin intact. While the core dries (if it hasn't been wet long, you will only need to replace the damaged portion), you can repair the damage to the panel of skin. Reglue the repaired skin to the core, then grind a 12-to-1 bevel around the cut line and bond the piece back in place.

KEEL AND RUDDER DAMAGE

Unless you are an extremely timid navigator, eventually you find yourself coming to a rude stop as you unexpectedly run out of water. In such events, it is generally the keel or the rudder that takes the brunt of the impact. When the bottom is ooze or sand, little if any harm is done, but fetching up against solid granite or jagged coral is likely to result in serious trauma.

Scrape and gouge repairs to a fiberglass keel and rudder are no different than on other parts of the hull, except that damage to the keel or rudder should make you suspicious. Because of the lever effect, even a modest impact near the bottom of an underwater appendage applies off-the-scale stresses at the attachment points; fin keels can break the hull like the pull ring on a pop-top can, and rudders can tear free of their stocks. Even an encapsulated full keel, less at risk at the bilge, may deform from the inertia and split, letting seawater into the ballast cavity. All repairs to keel and rudder should include a thorough inspection for collateral damage.

WEEPING KEEL

A grounded boat lifted and dropped by even modest wave action hits the bottom with the force of a pile driver. If even a fist-size rock is under the hammering keel, the bottom laminate may be distorted enough to split. Such damage is likely to go unnoticed unless you look for it, or until the water intrusion causes iron ballast to swell and deform the keel.

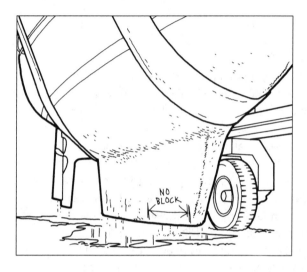

1 Examine the bottom of the keel while the boat is in the hoist and mark where you want yard workers to place the blocks so your access to any suspect areas won't be obstructed.

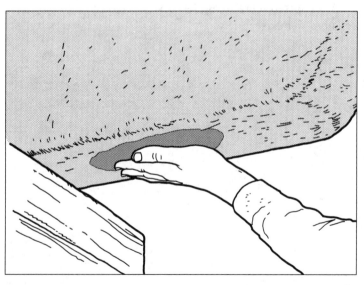

2 Scrape, scrub, and rinse the keel, and let it dry completely. Now examine it with eye and finger for any signs of lingering wetness. Weeping that persists for more than a day indicates a crack in the keel laminate.

3 Grind away the bottom paint in the wet area. The crack should become visible.

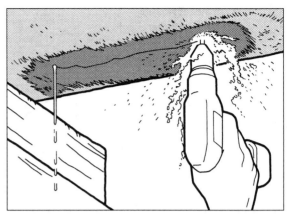

4 Find the ends of the crack and use a battery- or hand-powered drill to drill a 3/16-inch hole at each end. These holes mark the break, relieve stress that might lengthen the crack, and allow the cavity to drain. Don't use a plugged-in drill because water may pour out when you puncture the skin.

5 Grind a V along the crack line and beyond each end. The bottom of the V should reach the last layer of laminate, and the sides should have a 12-to-1 bevel.

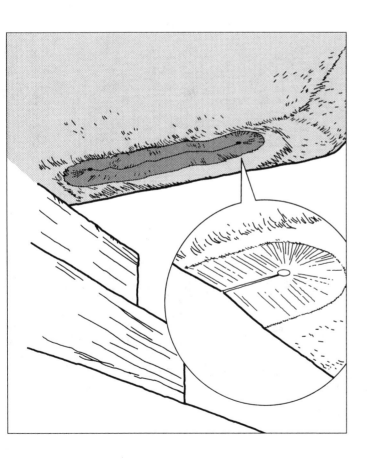

6 Laminate the repair using epoxy resin for a better bond and better resilience to future groundings.

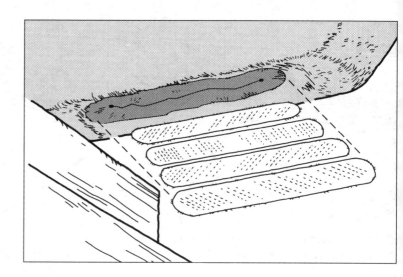

7 If a cracked keel is a recurring problem, grind the entire bottom of the keel and a few inches up the side, then add several additional laminates of glass cloth. You can also strengthen the keel by adding additional laminates from inside if you have interior access.

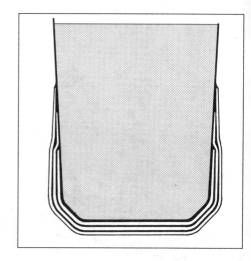

INTEGRAL FUEL TANKS

SOME OF THE SPACE INSIDE A MOLDED KEEL is often used for tankage. This is fine as long as there is actually a tank, but occasionally, to save money, designers or builders have opted for what is known as an integral tank—the designated space in the keel is simply partitioned off from the ballast area and given a fiberglass top. In such cases, a crack in the keel in the tank area may weep fuel.

Permanent repairs will not be possible without emptying the tank and removing all fuel residue from the fiberglass in the area around the crack. The best way of dealing with an integral tank is to replace it with a proper tank; the type will depend on the liquid it is to hold. Cut and grind away the top of the integral tank and steam clean the cavity, then take the dimensions to your tank builder. Meanwhile you can repair the crack in the skin.

KEEL/CENTERBOARD PIVOT PROBLEMS

In a keel/centerboard boat, the pivot pin usually passes through the stub keel, sealed on each end by a plug of mish-mash (a putty made from resin and chopped fiberglass). Leaks around the pivot only rarely get inside the boat because the space in the stub keel, presumably filled with ballast, is usually sealed off from the interior of the hull. A leaking pivot pin is nevertheless a serious problem, especially if the ballast is iron or steel. Rusting steel can expand with enough force to split the confining fiberglass. Even if the ballast is lead, water inside the ballast cavity can freeze during winter storage and rupture the hull.

How do you know if the pivot pin is leaking? If the area around the pin stays wet for days after the boat is hauled (check *inside* the trunk), water is weeping out of the keel and the pin is leaking.

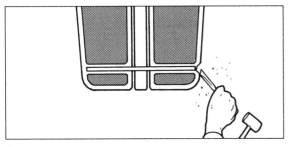

1 Drill and chip out the putty covering both ends of the pivot pin. Take the weight off the pin by supporting the centerboard, and tap out of the keel stub. Remove the centerboard or shift it out of the way.

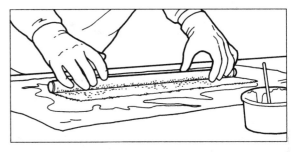

2 Because of hollows in the keel stub, drilling the hole oversize and filling it with epoxy is often impractical. Wax the pin *heavily*. Wet out a piece of light cloth with epoxy and roll it onto the pin to form a fiberglass tube. When the epoxy cures, slip the pin out of the tube.

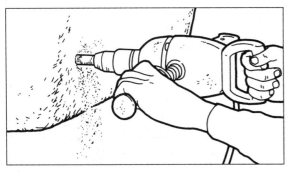

3 Enlarge the hole in the keel stub to the outside diameter of the tube. This can be the most difficult part of the job if the hole is large and the ballast is iron.

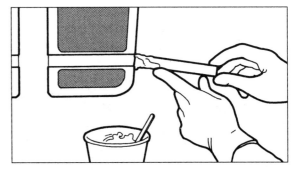

4 Cut the tube into two shorter pieces and epoxy them into the keel. Use epoxy thickened with colloidal silica, and take great care to get a good seal at each end of the tubes where they pass through the fiberglass. Reinstall the pin and seal each end with epoxy putty.

A bolted-on fin keel or skeg functions like a pry-bar when it hits something, deflecting the hull laminate into an S-shape as the front of the fin tries to tear away from the hull and the back tries to drive into the interior.

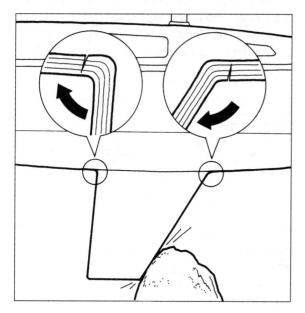

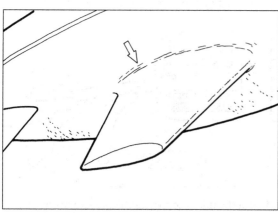

2 Don't confuse gelcoat cracks with laminate damage. Gelcoat often cracks around the fin or skeg because it is more brittle than the underlying laminate. Repair the gelcoat cracks to protect the laminate from water intrusion.

1 Check the hull, both inside and outside, all around the base of the fin. Expect ruptures to be in the outside laminates forward of the fin and in the inside laminates aft. Splits beside the fin can be inside or outside depending on how the fin was stressed.

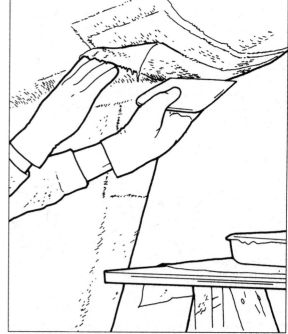

3 Hull damage around a fin almost always signals inadequate laminate strength. After you grind open and repair all damaged laminate, add additional layers of fiberglass to strengthen the hull in the affected area.

DAMAGED RUDDER

In order to neither float nor sink when the boat heels, a sailboat rudder needs to have nearly neutral buoyancy. That means fiberglass rudders are usually foam filled or hollow. Unfortunately, too many are also so lightly built that the slightest brush with anything more solid than a jellyfish breaks the skin. Weeping rudders are even more common than weeping keels, and water inside your rudder is almost certainly doing damage.

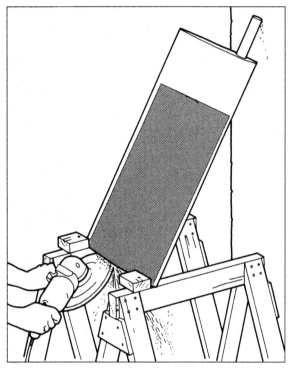

1 If you have a weep anywhere on your rudder, the entire rudder may be full of water, but it will only drain out to the level of the crack. It is almost always a good idea to grind a hole in the lowest part of the skin to allow complete drainage.

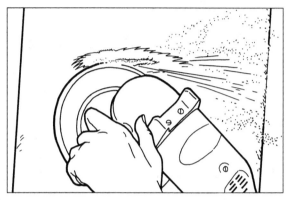

2 Grind the damaged area open to expose enough of the core to determine what it is and whether it is saturated.

3 If the core is saturated, you should have some success in drying it by removing the rudder and drilling a pattern of $3/16$-inch holes all the way through it on about 6-inch centers. Put the rudder on sawhorses in an enclosed area and place a small electric heater beneath it. After a few days drill a couple of test holes to see if all the core is drying. If closer spaced holes seem necessary, removing one of the skins may be easier.

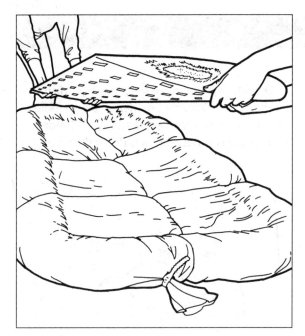

4 When the core is dry, tape the holes closed on one side. "Nestle" that side of the rudder into sand-filled garbage bags, then put it back on the horses, supported as close to the ends as possible to keep from compressing the skin against the core.

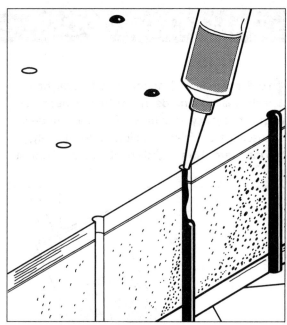

5 Mix epoxy to catsup consistency with colloidal silica and inject each hole until it refuses to accept more or until epoxy appears in the adjacent holes. Fill every hole, working quickly to fill all the voids before the epoxy begins to set. A slow hardener is helpful.

6 Position the rudder in the sandbag "nest" and weight the top surface with sandbags to compress the skins against the core.

7 When the epoxy has fully cured, regrind the damaged area and the drain hole and repair both with lay-ups of fiberglass cloth and epoxy.

Resin doesn't attach to metal very well, so to keep a rudder from spinning on the stock, it is usually built around a metal framework welded to the stock. Done well, this provides a strong and trouble-free assembly, but too often the framework is little more than two or three metal straps or rods spot-welded to the stock. When (not if) these welds break, the rudder swings freely.

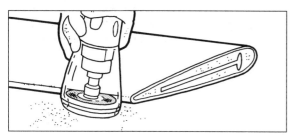

1 Fiberglass rudders are almost always built in two halves and glued together over the stock assembly and the core. Split the seam with a circular saw or rotary tool (dremel) and separate the two halves. Making the cut to one side will make reassembly easier.

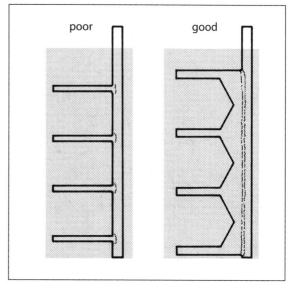

2 Remove the broken framework and have a new one constructed that attaches to the stock for almost the full length of the rudder.

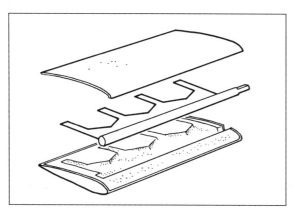

3 Relieve the foam core to fit the new framework and join the two halves with epoxy thickened to mayonnaise consistency with colloidal silica. Clamp or weight the halves together until the epoxy cures fully, then grind a bevel on the cut line and laminate the two halves together.

Grounding an external lead keel is less likely to damage the hull, but the keel may be deformed by the impact.

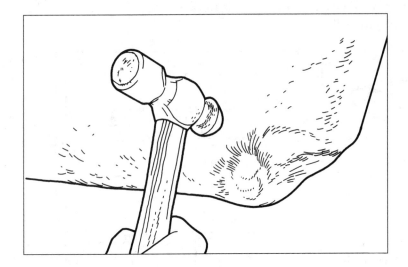

1 Use the round end of a ball-peen hammer to reshape the lead. You are trying to "push" the displaced lead back in shape; be careful not to shear the bulge.

2 Remove high spots with a body plane or a sharp block plane. Lubricate the lead with petroleum jelly before you plane it.

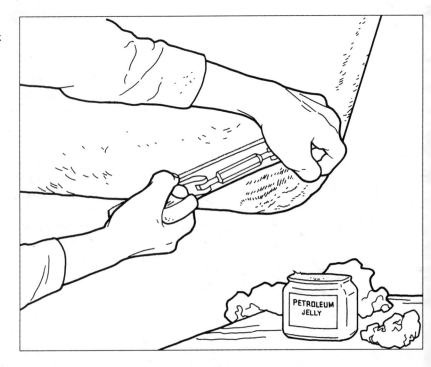

PETROLEUM JELLY

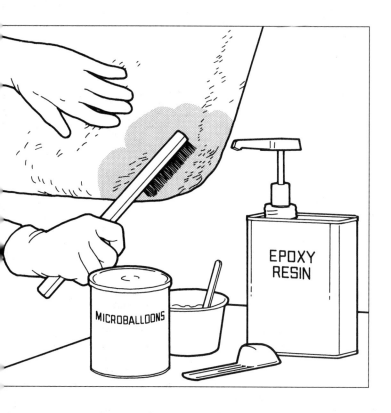

3 Fill low spots with epoxy and microballons. First remove the petroleum jelly and any other contaminants with acetone, and wire brush the lead. Wet the lead with epoxy, then wire brush it again to expose fresh lead to the epoxy without exposing it to the air. Thicken your epoxy to peanut butter consistency with microballoons (there is no blister risk here) and flush-fill the depressions.

4 Sand the entire area after the filler cures and coat it with unthickened epoxy, sanding the wet surface to expose fresh lead to the epoxy. Give the repair two additional coats of epoxy, then sand and paint.

INDEX

NOTE ON TERMINOLOGY FOR UK READERS

Many American terms in this book will be readily understandable by UK readers. However, one or two may cause confusion and for this reason we give below the UK equivalent, which readers may find helpful.

US	UK
bungs	dowels
cabinetry	joinery
centreboard trunks	centreboard casing
dead frames	either internal or external frames, according to sense
deadlight	portlight (often overlaid acrylic type, in the case of replacement windows)
Gel-O	jelly
MEK	Methyl Ethyl Ketone
mineral spirits	white spirit or turpentine
polysulfide	polysulphide
System Three	SP Systems
through-hull fittings	skin fittings

LIST OF SUPPLIERS/MANUFACTURERS

(Correct at the time of writing. For a comprehensive listing see *Sells Marine Market* or Marine Factors/Discount Yacht Chandlers in the yachting magazines.)

BOAT GRAPHICS (NAMES, LOGOS, AND TRIM STRIPES, ETC.)

AWS Custom Graphics, 79 Baltimore Road, Perry Bar, Birmingham B42 1DG.

Istron Graphics, 56 Lower Park Road, Brightlingsea, Colchester, Essex CD7 0JX.

CHANDLERY (GENERAL)

Davey & Co., 4 Oak Industrial Park, Great Dunmow, Essex CM6 1XN.

Plastimo (UK) Ltd., School Lane, Chandlers Ford Industrial Estate, Eastleigh, Hants S05 3DG.

Simpson Lawrence Ltd., 218-228 Edmiston Drive, Glasgow G51 2YT.

Vetus UK Ltd., Greasley Street, Bulwell, Nottingham NG6 8NJ.

CLEANING MATERIALS

Farecla Products, 3 Crane Mead, Ware, Herts SG12 9PY.

Hawk Marine and Industrial Products, 160 Tower Street, Brightlingsea, Essex CO7 0AW.

Wynn's Marine, Wynn Oil (UK) Ltd., Thames Court, 2 Richfield Avenue, Reading RG1 8EQ.

CORE MATERIALS/GLASSCLOTH

Anglo Swiss Aluminium Co. (Airex), Mander House, Mander Centre, Wolverhampton WV1 3ND.

ATL Adhesives Ltd., 160 Tower Street, Brightlingsea, Essex CO7 0AW.

Baltek, Green Dragon House, 64 High Street, Croydon, Surrey CR0 9XN.

Barracuda Technologies, 1 Eastville Close, Gloucester GL4 7SJ.

Courtaulds Advanced Materials, Fothergill Engineered Fabrics, PO Box 1, Summit, Littleborough, Lancs OL15 9QP.

GRP Factors, 2 First Avenue, Bluebridge Industrial Estate, Halstead, Essex CO9 2EX.

FASTENINGS (SCREWS/BOLTS, ETC.)

Anglia Stainless Steel Ltd., Shepherds Grove Industrial Estate, Stanton, Suffolk IP31 2AR.

Fastpack Ltd., PO Box 16, York YO1 3YX.

Felix Fasteners Ltd., 27 Amory Street, Alton, Hants.

FITTINGS (CUSTOM FABRICATED)

Moyle Castings & Marine, Dept. 23, 73 Walton Road, Woking, Surrey GU21 5DP.

Oliver Dale, Restronguet Barton Workshop, Mylor, Falmouth, Cornwall TR11 5SP.

E.C. Smith & Sons, Units H and J, Kingsway Industrial Estate, Kingsway, Luton, Beds LU1 1LP.

Steeline Ltd., 2 Long Acre Close, Holbrook, Sheffield S19 5FR.

LINING/INSULATION MATERIALS

A& B Textiles, Unit 20, Pier Road Industrial Estate, Gillingham, Kent ME7 1RZ.

Fibre-Tech Insulation Ltd., Unit 5a, Butts Farm, Butts Lane, Fowlmere, Royston, Herts SG8 7SL.

Halyard (M & I) Whaddon Business Park, Southampton Road, Whaddon, Nr Salisbury SP5 3HF.

Kooltherm Insulation Products Ltd., PO Box 3, Charlestown Works, Charlestown, Glossop, Derbyshire SK13 8LE.

Toomery and Hayter Ltd., 74 Green Road, Winton, Bournemouth BH9 1EB.

PAINT SUPPLIERS/MANUFACTURERS

Aquarius Marine Coatings Ltd., Cobbs Quay, Hamworthy, Poole, Dorset BH15 4EL.

Awlgrip (distributors) Marineware, Unit 6, Crosshouse Centre, Southampton SO14 5GZ.

Blakes Marine Paints Ltd., Harbour Road, Gosport, Hants PO12 1BQ.

Graf Epoxy UK Ltd., 22 High Gate, Cherry Burton, Beverley, North Humberside HU17 7RR

Geedon Marine Ltd., Commerce Park, Whitehall Road, Colchester, Essex CO2 8HX.

International Paints Ltd., 24 - 30, Canute Road, Southampton SO14 3PB.

W.S. Jenkins, Jeco Works, Tariff Road, Tottenham, London N17 0EN.

Llewellyn Ryland Ltd., 24 Haden Street, Birmingham B12 9DB.

Skipper UK Ltd., The Boathouse, Bitterne Triangle, Southampton SP18 1FZ.

Wastnage Ltd., 8 Springfield Industrial Estate, Burnham-on-Crouch, Essex.

PAINT STRIPPERS (GRP)

Skarsten Manufacturing Co. Ltd., 1 Cronin Courtyard, Corby, Northants NN18 8AG.

RESINS

B & K Resins Ltd., Ashgrove Estate, Ashgrove Road, Bromley, Kent BR1 4TH.

Bondaglass-Voss Ltd., 158 - 160 Ravenscroft Road, Beckenham, Kent BR3 4TW.

Scott Bader Co. Ltd., Wollaston, Wellingborough, Northants NN9 7RL.

S P Systems Ltd., Love Lane, Cowes, Isle of Wight PO31 7EU.

Wessex Resins and Adhesives Ltd., Cupernham House, Cupernham Lane, Romsey, Hants SO51 7LF.

Stag Polymers and Sealants Ltd., Tavistock Road, West Drayton, Middlesex UB7 7RA.

SEALANTS

Marine and Industrial Sealants Ltd., Keepers Cottage, Westwick Hill, Westwick, Norfolk NR10 5BQ.

Sowester Ltd. (distributors of "Sika" products), Stinsford Road, Nuffield Industrial Estate, Poole, Dorset BH17 7SW.

TIMBER AND PLYWOOD

Amalgamated Hardwoods Ltd., Englemere Sawmills, London Road, Ascot, Berks SL5 8DG.

Robbins Timber, Merrywood Road, Bedminster, Bristol BS3 1DX.

Bruynzeel Multipanel (UK) Ltd., East Industrial Estate, 6 Freebournes Road, Witham, Essex CM8 3UN.

WATER/WASTE/FUEL TANKS

Seaflex Ltd., Samuel Whites, Cowes, Isle of Wight PO30 7DU.

Tek-Tanks, Unit 5b, Station Approach, Four Marks, Alton, Hants GU34 5HN.

WINDOW SEALS

Cherry's Chandlery, 934 Wimborne Road, Moordown, Bournemouth, Dorset BH9 2DH.

WINDOWS AND WINDOW PANELS

Display Developments Ltd., 22 Gilbert Road, Belvedere, Kent.

Branchsound Ltd., Unit 9, Springfield Industrial Estate, Burnham-on-Crouch, Essex CM0 8TE.

Houdini Marine Windows, Hallmark Industrial Estate, Southminster, Essex CM0 7EH.

Eagle Boat Windows, 28 Arthur Street, Barnoldswick, Lancashire BB8 5JZ.

Trend Marine Products, Sutton Road, Catfield, Gt. Yarmouth, Norfolk NR29 5BG.

Published by Adlard Coles Nautical
an imprint of A & C Black Publishers Ltd
38 Soho Square, London W1D 3HB
www.adlardcoles.com

First published in the USA in 1996 by International Marine under the title
Sailboat Hull and Deck Repair

First published in hardback in the UK in 1998 under the title *Hull and Deck Repair*

First UK paperback published in 2008 by Adlard Coles Nautical

ISBN 978-1-4081-0002-8

A CIP catalogue record for this book is available from the British Library.

Printed and bound in the USA.
Illustrations in Chapters 1, 2, 6, and 7 by Jim Sollers.
Illustrations in Chapters 3, 4, and 5 by Rob Groves.

DON CASEY credits the around-the-world-voyage of Robin Lee Graham, featured in National Geographic in the late sixties, with opening his eyes to the world beyond the shoreline. After graduating from the University of Texas he moved to south Florida, where he began to spend virtually all his leisure time messing about in boats.

In 1983 he abandoned a career in banking to devote more time to cruising and writing. His work combining these two passions soon began to appear in many popular sailing and boating magazines. In 1986 he co-authored *Sensible Cruising: The Thoreau Approach*, an immediate best-seller and the book responsible for pushing many would-be cruisers over the horizon. He is also author of *This Old Boat,* a universally praised guide that has led thousands of boatowners through the process of turning a rundown production boat into a first-class yacht, and of *Sailboat Refinishing*.

When not writing or off cruising, he can be found sailing on Florida's Biscayne Bay.